PRAISE FOR
UNASSISTED

"This memoir is a reflection on living a fully engaged and an intentional life. Erin Stammer's authentic, empowered voice takes the reader on a literary journey where we find love and joy in the most unexpected places and most difficult situations. Full of emotional truths and hard-won wisdom, resilience and grace, *Unassisted* is a perfect book club book."

—RUTH WARINER, author of *The Sound of Gravel*

"Erin is a tremendous storyteller. Her memoir is compelling, her writing lyrical, almost as if we are caught in a dream that is her struggle to right size her life, when faced with one of the greatest challenges of her career. As we read about the enchantment of her early childhood, the pain of her adolescence and the midlife events that bring forth all the things that she never resolved, we stagger along with her, and we maintain hope. In the end, this book is about finding home, where we can not only survive, but thrive."

—TOM HALLMAN, Pulitzer Prize winner and
senior reporter for *The Oregonian*

"Home is not always a place of love and nurture; often it's a place where we are uncertain and wary. And similar to Erin's story, many of us find a way to overcome, heal, and forgive. In *Unassisted*, readers are taken on a journey of a woman who despite the episodic dysfunction of her childhood, became the strong woman she was born to be."

—STEPHANIE PLYMALE, author of *American Daughter* and
CEO of Heritage School of Interior Design

A Memoir about Self-Discovery
and the Meaning of Home

UNASSISTED

ERIN J. STAMMER

RIVER GROVE
BOOKS

Published by River Grove Books
Austin, TX
www.rivergrovebooks.com

Distributed by River Grove Books

Design and composition by Greenleaf Book Group
Cover design by Greenleaf Book Group
©iStockphoto.com/Photo2008

Publisher's Cataloging-in-Publication data is available.

Print ISBN: 978-1-63299-321-2

eBook ISBN: 978-1-63299-322-9

First Edition

To Camille, Cole, Gunnar, and Ava, from whom,
by mothering you, I've learned to accept countless
human foibles, including my own.

"What matters in life is not what happens to you but what you remember and how you remember it."

—GABRIEL GARCÍA MÁRQUEZ

CONTENTS

ACKNOWLEDGMENTS

The list of family, friends, lovers, mentors, and guides who have influenced my life to date—who helped shape my first impressions and worldview; who taught me right from wrong, how to love, and how to forgive; who made me laugh, cry, and everything in between—is a long one. There are cats, dogs, turtles, and parakeets included. There are cobblestoned streets, art galleries, sandy beaches, and mountain lakes in my rearview mirror. There are those who spoke to me in a foreign tongue and those who only could clap their hands and coo.

There are memories of campfires, windstorms, stuffy classrooms, playgrounds, vegetable gardens, old pickups, and sourdough pancakes hot off the stove. I am the sum of my own spirit plus all of you and all that I've observed, all that I've touched and experienced.

Thank you, Mom, for bringing me into the world after a lobster dinner and a nip of scotch. Thank you, Nancy and Magen, my rocks from age five to eighteen. Thank you to my dearest friends for the past twenty-two years since we met dropping our kids off at Child's View Montessori. You know who you are. Thank you for sharing motherhood with me. Thank you to my siblings, Caitlin and Josh, for being my best friends since birth. Thank you to my favorite Brown professor, Meera Viswanathan, for lighting up the room with your erudition and wit. Thank you to Amy, Sarah, Linda, and Catherine, who shared your families and homes with me in New England when I needed you, and them, most. Thank you to the men I've loved who challenged me, cared for me, and made my heart burst into flames.

Most of all, thank you to Jay, my life partner, who, like no other, has always faced in the same direction as myself, and who has always believed in me.

JOBLESS

The summer I finished my master's degree in healthcare administration, I wasn't looking all that hard for a job. Both Jay and I had become unemployed during the Great Recession. He first, calling me from his BlackBerry on a Tuesday afternoon in 2008 as he drove across the bridge from Vancouver, Washington, into Portland. I could barely hear him. Naturally quiet, he also had his window open to the late August sun and freeway air.

"Well," he said, his voice still melting me two years into our relationship. "I got laid off today." I wanted to reach out and touch his face. I closed my eyes and opened them again, glancing at the four walls of my office and my inbox full of unread email.

Three weeks later I had convinced him to move his two children into my house with my own two children. I couldn't see the sense in his continuing to pay rent on his set of rooms in the house off Vista Street, which clung to the side of the hill like a mountain climber taking a breath.

Only a few months later I was driving into work, when,

stalled by traffic on Highway 217, I checked my own company-issued BlackBerry. The president's administrative assistant had prematurely sent out a company-wide email intended for later that day. It read that we had all lost our jobs, in case we did not understand what was said to us when we were called into the only conference room that would accommodate everyone and received the message that first froze us, then sent us reeling. Except that we had not yet been called into that conference room; that meeting had been intended for later that day.

Fifteen years I had worked for Textron. It was my family, my identity, my haven. I had not been without work since I was hired by Systran Financial at the age of twenty-three, and when Systran was acquired by Textron Financial in 1998, it doubled in size, creating more opportunities for me every year. I was an institution there. No one questioned me, whether I was at my desk or downstairs having coffee. I was invited to most meetings, whether I needed to be there or not. The company had even been paying for my master's degree, since I had convinced them that it would help me know my customer base better. We were lenders to healthcare entities—nursing homes, hospitals, endoscopy equipment manufacturers, and so on. I wanted to be able to dig into my customers' industry so that when I was sharing a steak dinner with the CEO of a small hospital system, I could—in theory, at least—hear and respond to their challenges and their long-term strategy. I wanted to be that ideal lender who "gets it."

In the end Textron gave me what the company thought

was an ample severance package and a reluctant nod to work another six months, until March 2009. I appreciated the gesture. Although I tend to be calm in a storm, I knew I needed more time to accept my loss and adjust to the impact to my family. I needed time to come up with a plan. As the recession gained momentum, everything was crashing around us, and I watched my retirement fund shrink slowly, until it was devastatingly low. Gone, too, was the assurance that I'd always be moving forward, gaining in every respect, acquiring. That feeling seemed like a distant memory. I looked around and saw only what would have to wait: the beach house I wanted to own, the nicer car, the new front door, the backyard deck.

Still, Jay and I, both raised by parents of modest means, knew what it meant to buckle down. We sat together at the kitchen table and wrote down what we could reduce or eliminate. We moved our priorities around on a spreadsheet like chess pieces. Later we told the four children over dinner how certain things would change, that it would be tight for a while. We didn't know how long. There were few questions. The kids trusted us, though this combined family thing was still new. We had ensured that every one of them had their own bedroom because we wanted them each to have a space to which they could escape and be uniquely themselves. Jay and I gave up our master bedroom to accomplish this and moved ourselves into the family room in the basement.

Jay found contract work with Portland Public Schools just

as my extended time at Textron was ending. I knew his ego
had been wounded by the layoff from the bank where he had
worked. It seemed he was expendable and that others mattered more. I hugged him, and we talked about starting over,
because that was how it was. Though we were both in our
early forties, he had been set back a decade in terms of the
level of job and salary he could find. We were humbled by
the limited opportunities. I tried not to think about it.

We had agreed that I would finish my master's program
over the summer and we'd live cautiously off my severance
package. Surely I would find work in the fall. Perhaps the
recession would abate by then.

That summer there were so many adjustments that my
heart began to fray at the edges. My two children, Camille
and Gunnar, had entered an age where the tight mother-child
bond had started to unravel. I felt their unfolding separation,
their determination to become who they would be without
me. It was no longer easy to get them to join me on mundane
trips to the grocery store or to go on weekend family outings.
They pouted and argued when we spent an afternoon at the
Saturday Market. One wanted to take the MAX—the light-
rail system—the other to go by car. They chose different food
vendors two blocks apart. They were hungry at different times.
Camille no longer found Gunnar's antics funny and pretended
to not know him. Neither wanted to hold my hand.

I was also becoming someone else: a stepmother. It was
not a role I stepped into gracefully. I had private tantrums,
petty anger at having to share with Jay and his children what

I had built as a single mom with my two offspring. There were awkward attempts to understand my stepchildren, so different from my own two kids. Jay and I spent late nights in bed, especially on weekends after a few martinis or a bottle of wine, trying to figure out how to merge our families—what to allow, where to give or take back, and who could arbiter what with whom. Discipline was a big topic, as were expectations of mutual respect, family time, chores. It was like starting over after I had so finely honed my own motherhood. I wanted to scream and escape at once.

And I was pregnant.

When Jay and I first started dating, he had told me that if he met someone new after his divorce, and she did not have children and wanted to, he would certainly oblige. I remember looking at him over the dimly lit table at Caffe Mingo, a fresh charcuterie board between us, our glasses filled with Barolo. In those days, we were deep into exploring each other's minds and bodies. We wanted to know each other completely, as if this might help us avoid the mistakes we made with our first spouses.

"Why?" I asked.

"Well, because it would be something she had not experienced yet. I would not want to withhold that from her," he said. His answer seemed well rehearsed.

"What if I wanted to have another child?" I looked at Jay coyly through the candles flickering over the coppa, pickles, and prosciutto. Since giving birth to my first child, I had wanted at least two more. To be honest I wanted five children. I had once wanted to be a stay-at-home mother, too, but I had long given up on that fantasy. I was not the type to seek out a man who would comfortably provide for me. It unnerved me to consider it. Would he want an impeccable house and banana bread in the oven when he came home at night? Would I feel compelled to make love with him even when I wasn't in the mood? Would I hesitate to ask him for money so I could buy a new dress? I had taken too many college feminism courses to avoid these dark thoughts.

"Really?" Jay asked. I could see him adjusting internally, careful with each word, avoiding conflict at all costs. As I grew to know him better, I recognized this not as a weakness but as the sign of a person willing to see the other side and to get comfortable with it. This was how he loved.

"Well, if that's what you want, sweetheart, then we could do that. We better get started, though." He grinned. "For one thing, I need to reopen the swim lanes."

I scoffed. A reverse vasectomy was a walk in the park compared to childbirth. To me the greater obstacle seemed our age. We were both thirty-nine. Yet our relationship was still too new to consider bringing a child into the world, despite my longings. This was a topic that would not be revisited for a couple of years.

I was forty-one before we both felt ready. Jay visited the doctor for some repairs and I had gone to see an acupuncturist because I had entered perimenopause. Two years into our relationship, I discovered I was pregnant. I was elated, but I think Jay was terrified. I reassured him that I had had two easy pregnancies. He seemed unconvinced but stalwart. We would do this: It would be yours, mine, and ours.

Toward the end of August, I was sitting at my makeshift desk in our living room. Space had become a premium as we now had six people living in 1,960 square feet. My cell phone rang, an unknown number. For several weeks I had been sending around my resume, asking for introductions, surfing Indeed, LinkedIn, and the websites of companies I was interested in. Positions in finance had completely disappeared; there was nothing at all. In that first year of the recession it was as if a plague had descended on finance and banking. I wondered who was still doing the work. Did they show up at the office each day, sick in the pit of their stomach, as they walked by empty cubicles to their own desks, the ghosts of laid-off co-workers raising coffee cups at them in a silent cheer?

I would receive my diploma in healthcare administration from Portland State that December. Why not utilize it? Still, the idea of changing from working in finance to working in healthcare was daunting. How would my resume be received? Would I have to start at the bottom? What if my master's degree wasn't enough for me to be successful? As it turned out, my resume made its way from my mentor at a Medicaid insurer in Portland to a contact of hers whom I had met for an informational interview to another friend who worked for a large hospital system in Oregon. And from there, it landed on Wendy Sullivan's desk.

Wendy, as I could tell from our very first phone conversation, was a real "spark plug," as my mother would say. She was passionate about a hundred thousand things, full of fire, loving and inclusive, smart as a whip, and had worked her whole life in healthcare. As I came to know her, I admired her grit, her seeming ability to put up mental walls so she could move on from the painful situations that presented themselves regularly in her industry, and be just as gay and serene the next day as she was five minutes before being faced with them.

"Erin!" Wendy practically yelled into the phone. "I'm sitting here with your amazing-looking resume, and I would love to talk to you about a position here at ElderHome in Stratford United Place."

I glanced down at the evidence of my efforts to find a job on my desk, a stack of contacts and notes about people, positions, and places. ElderHome in Stratford United Place was not ringing any bells. Honesty seemed best while she was still going on about my "stellar" resume on the other end of the phone.

"Wendy, I am so glad you called and would very much like to speak to you about the position. I have sent out several queries. Could you possibly remind me of which position this is?" I bit my lip as I paused.

Wendy laughed, her voice as delightful as birds chattering in a blossoming tree. "No worries. Let me go over this with you, and then we can see if you have any interest and possibly come in for an interview?"

I nodded, although she could not see me do so. I was grateful to hear the word "interview." I had not managed to snag any interviews up to that point, and doom was lurking in the corners of my mind, like cobwebs multiplying on the ceiling. By my rough calculations my severance would last only until the end of November, and Jay's contractor salary would barely cover the mortgage and groceries. I had pulled both my kids out of private school, but they were still playing club soccer and needed new school clothes. Their father's child support check was infrequent and a small amount. For years I had supported us as a single mom on a salary I had come to take for granted. The fact of my unemployment had become a fragile cliff, threatening to break loose and obliterate the landscape of my life. I had to find a job.

Wendy's call that day felt like a cup of water handed out by a friendly volunteer halfway through a 10k race. By the time I hung up, I had a piece of paper with the date, time, and address of the assisted living facility where my interview would take place the following week. My heart raced. The cliff was holding together with tangled vines, disaster receding.

2

THE INTERVIEW

The morning of the interview, I woke up to a familiar routine: shower, have coffee, check phone and email, do hair and makeup, dress, find jewelry. I recalled my years rising at 3 a.m. to catch a flight to Atlanta or Fayetteville, Riverside or Philadelphia, arriving early afternoon on the East Coast in time for a tour of my client's home-health or rehab facility, hospital, or outpatient care clinic. There would be formal conversations with the president and CFO in their offices, followed by dinner at the most celebrated restaurants in town, with inane chatter over our meal, lots of agreeing on things, and finding common ground. Money was flowing from my shop to theirs. The operational performance may have been wobbly, but that was healthcare; I had come to know the weaknesses, the pressures of the industry well.

For the interview at Stratford, I had rehearsed my background and knowledge over and over, incorporating it into the story of why I was suitable to run an assisted living facility (ALF) and a medical clinic, with no prior experience in either.

After all, I had been in so many of these places I knew how they operated. I believed I knew the demographic of ALF residents and patients. Looking back, I think my naïveté must have shone on my face the day I first walked into the facility, and remained there for the eighteen months I stayed. I wore it like a badge on a Girl Scout's vest. Put into words, my demeanor might have proclaimed, "Scared, trusting, but brave."

ElderHome in Stratford United Place, or Stratford as it was known to all of us who worked, lived, and visited there, was not in an area of town I spent much time in. I looked at Google Maps on my computer at home and printed the directions, leaving ten minutes earlier than the time suggested. As I drove, I wondered if I had drunk one cup of coffee too many. My hands gripped the wheel, and I saw the telltale signs of my Raynaud's purpling my fingertips. It was much too early in the season for symptoms of the circulatory disease that chilled my extremities. I took a few deep pranayama breaths, as I had learned in yoga.

The gray tone of the city blurred buildings and the river into a flattened relief as I drove across the Fremont Bridge and took the exit into a neighborhood of contrasts. Old turn-of-the-century houses beamed with the pride of fresh paint, begonias in planter boxes on the porch, and newer Priuses parked in the driveway, while other homes had fallen into disrepair. An underfed cat pawed at the torn screen of one front door; weeds sprouted from cracks in another walkway near a broken window patched by cardboard and duct tape. Construction loomed on every corner.

Google took me down one street and then over to another, avoiding the main drag that I would eventually come to follow by rote. I saw a hipster couple walking with their hand in each other's back pocket, bodies close. He smoked a cigarette with his free hand and adjusted the knit cap on his head, smiling at his girlfriend over his goatee. She laughed at something he said, her mouth wide, her narrow hips and long hair swaying jauntily in the morning breeze. On the next block, I observed an older man standing on the steps of his house, his hands clasped together, the sleeves of his worn plaid coat hanging to his knuckles. He looked as if he had nowhere to go.

I parked on a side street in front of Stratford. I was glad for my nondescript 1998 Volvo station wagon with its dings and scrapes. Stepping out of the car, I noticed several people hovering on the corner. The sidewalk was littered with Big Gulps and candy wrappers from the local convenience store. The trees next to the sidewalk looked frail. I peered down at my feet, watching where I stepped.

When I walked into the assisted living facility, my mind was a tabula rasa, a blank slate. My internal conversation said, *Be open to whatever this might be.* The first and only time I had ever actually worked in a healthcare setting was in high school, when I interned as a researcher at Oregon Health and Science University. I was an introverted sixteen-year-old, with my head full of English novels and fantastical literature, obsessed with becoming as thin and unapproachable as a model in *W* magazine, whose oversize issues were flung across my twin bed every month when they arrived. The skeletal models drew my attention, their eyes circled in blue and their coifs groomed close to the skull. I cut out the images of their slack postures and pasted them on my walls and the fridge to remind me what I could look like if I just stopped eating.

As part of my internship I went into the stacks at the hospital looking for information on something called "HIV" or "AIDS." I wasn't sure which was right, but both would do, according to my supervisor, and I was to bring back photocopies of any study that referred to this newly documented disease. One afternoon one of the researchers suggested a field trip, as he was aware of my interest in Alzheimer's, something my maternal grandfather, Arno, had developed in the past year. I had learned the fundamentals of the disease—the neurotransmitters that decline, the first indications of memory loss, and what was to come later. I could already see my grandfather's eyes losing their intense glare and the weakness in his grip on my shoulder.

The researcher took me to the nursing home where his own grandmother was living. She had plain dementia, which just sounded like insanity to me. I had visions of sixteenth-century women tearing their hair out and denouncing their loved ones. Shortly after entering the nursing home (for that was what such facilities were called at that time), we encountered a woman with Huntington's chorea. This was the first time I had met someone with the disease. Her name was Helen. It was difficult to grasp her trembling hand, but she smiled at me when we finally connected palm to palm.

I remembered Helen and Arno as I looked discreetly around me in the entryway of Stratford United Place. The lighting was dim; frilly table lamps and mauve curtains were an attempt to appear homey. Scott Joplin's rag "The Entertainer" was being played on an untuned piano in some larger room down the hall. Residents gathered in groups of twos and threes nearby, as they rested in wheelchairs and leaned against walkers. Their attire was eclectic but exhibited flair, individuality, and pride. Out-of-season hats, mismatched socks, and bejeweled cropped tees competed with hot-pink track suits, cracked leather coats, and flower-patterned housecoats with pockets full of used tissues and bottles of pills. The residents maneuvered their power mobility devices to more carefully assess what the front door had spit in: me.

As I spoke with the receptionist at the front desk, I caught a faint scent of sweat and disdain. I could feel eyes sizing up my navy blue suit and matching pumps, my "interview uniform" which seemed overly formal in the setting. I turned to walk to the waiting room and smiled at two women near its doorway.

"Hello," I endeavored. The younger woman's hair was artfully arranged with extensions and fuchsia accent curls, and her big brown eyes appraised me through thick glasses. Her brightly manicured nails tapped at the handles of her friend's wheelchair. She couldn't have been more than thirty. She looked at me mildly, curious.

"Heyyyyyy," she said, her lower lip pouting a bit. "Who are you?"

"Just here for an interview," I said warmly. The woman laughed a little, then whooped and pinched the other woman on her shoulder. I glanced down at her companion, who sat poised and pretty with a pink knit cap over her gray curly hair and a long pink robe buttoned up to her neck. I could have lifted her out of her wheelchair with one hand. She looked straight ahead over her spectacles, didn't even react to the pinch.

"You're crazy if you want to work here!" hooted the younger woman. "Ain't that right, Miss Lonnie?" Miss Lonnie averted her gaze from the younger woman, who ignored her and turned back to me.

"I'm Karen," she said. "We got to go now. Very nice to meet you." As she turned and slowly pushed Miss Lonnie in the direction of the piano music, I saw her flip-flops slapping against the carpet. I walked into the waiting room and noticed several residents sitting in the available chairs, as if they, too, were waiting. There was a coffee table but no magazines. Every chair seemed wounded in some manner—a patchy spot or stain, a scratch or groove in the wood, wobbly legs, matted cushions. I chose to stand and pretended to inspect the art hanging indifferently on the walls. In my mind the words "stay cheerful" rose to the surface, like a fish I was trying to hook at the lake. I repeated it silently like a mantra.

These first impressions of Stratford would be joined by many others over the next eighteen months, impressions that were inevitably frustrating, heartening, disturbing, vexing, enlightening, and, yes, cheerful. My time at Stratford would turn out to be pivotal, turning my life upside down and prompting me to question a host of memories that were submerged in my consciousness—the intricacies of growing up, the family that formed me, marriage, parenting, and becoming the woman I had always believed I was supposed to be. That woman, I discovered, would never be the same after Stratford.

3

THE MIDDLE CHILD

I am the middle child, born fifteen months after my older sister, Caitlin, and fifteen months before my younger brother, Joshua. Being the middle child had certain advantages. I was never the focus of anyone's attention. It was assumed I would either trail behind my long-striding sister or gather up my brother's sticky hand as we shot forward into our day. I was rarely yelled at, and people were not likely to be looking for me. My mother dressed me like a porcelain doll, with two braids framing my face and in hand-sewn smocks, bright red tights, and Mary Janes. I would remain that way throughout the day, being a clean child who avoided messes, even as I awkwardly and energetically threw myself at life.

I never broke a bone and only occasionally skinned a wrist or knee, while my siblings fell off monkey bars in the playground, crashed from skateboards flying down hills at twenty-five miles per hour, and ripped tendons in their ankles while dancing in pointe shoes or tackling an opponent on the soccer field. One time I was playing an imaginary game with a couple of schoolmates in the pitch-black interior of the girl's restroom at our school gym, when I ran headlong into the Tampax dispenser. Its metal frame cut my left eyebrow in two. The scar it left is virtually the only one I possess on my body's external terrain.

You could say I led a cautious and very private life growing up.

When I was three, my unconventional parents answered an ad for a couple to manage a halfway house in Cambridge, Massachusetts. It was 1971, and we had been staying in a borrowed house in Northeast Portland due to the generosity of friends of my parents who had gone abroad to teach English.

The move came at an opportune time. That winter my father had been unemployed, and my mother took odd jobs providing childcare and editing students' school essays. For Christmas we decorated oranges with cloves to hang on the tree. In our stockings were chocolate coins covered in gold foil, and a Holly Hobbie doll, handmade by my mother to resemble each of us, with its own wardrobe. That year I remember my mother counting out food stamps at the grocery counter and all of us bundling up next to the fireplace to stay warm. The heat was never turned on.

My thirty-four-year-old mother had always loved new beginnings, any opportunity to toss away what no longer suited her and to reinvent herself. My father—her third husband—was young, only twenty-seven. Life was just beginning for him, and here he was, saddled with a spouse and three children under the age of five. But he was game for adventure. He was a poet, his MFA only recently completed at the University of Oregon. He could write anywhere. He found a part-time position teaching at an extension school of Harvard, while my mother narrowed our limited possessions down to only what would fit in the back of the brand-new Toyota Land Cruiser that my father proudly drove home and parked by the curb in front of our rental house. He had sold a few of his poems for the down payment. All three of us jumped on him, begging to be let inside. The fresh new-car smell was as exotic as avocados, as appealing as the scent of showers in the heat of summer.

Typically, I ended up seated in the middle. Secretly I didn't mind and only occasionally put up a fuss to make sure I could in fact pull *some* weight in the family. I felt safe in the car, lassoed by the black seat belts around our waists, my brother squirming constantly to some inner beat, my sister with her shredded baby blanket tucked up by her chin and her thumb in her mouth. I had my siblings to protect me from the fast-moving freeway outside where I imagined myself flying out like Supergirl in the event of a car accident. My mother had told all three of us enough stories of tragedies that befell children who did not wear their seat belts that I was almost certain of the inevitability of one occurring.

My fears were various, both unremarkable and unusual. I was afraid of the Easter Bunny, who in my mind was seven feet tall, sported pointy fangs, and was intent on stealing my Easter candy. Our neighbors had rabbits living outside in a wire-framed cage. I observed the animals' constant nibbling, their skittish ways, the rare moments they closed their eyes. One of my favorite Saturday morning cartoon characters was Bugs Bunny, a crafty and self-interested character who was forever up to tricks. I could not reconcile these impressions with a commercialized Easter Bunny with his smirky grin and soft white fur, bearing baskets full of sweets.

I was afraid of closets, yet I insisted it be pitch black when I slept, with the closet door, the blinds, and the bedroom door all closed. I was also fearful of what might be under the bed, so I never stowed things there or even looked under it. Years later my son Gunnar would behave in completely the opposite manner, falling asleep with the lights on and his door open, and tucking away all sorts of paraphernalia (clothing, old soccer cleats, Legos, stuffed monkeys and game cards, and a collection of rocks) under his bed in a vain attempt to hide from me what he was afraid I would give away or toss. He did not agree when I claimed he was "too old for that" or had "grown out of this." In his Peter Pan mind, he was never too grown up.

Anything with an engine generally upset me. Motorcycles, lawnmowers, generators. I shied away from loud and abrupt sounds, which ended my track career my freshman year of high school, despite breaking a fifteen-year-old record in the girl's 50 meters hurdles in my first meet. The gunshot that signaled the start of each race shattered me into a million pieces of pure fright; the only thing propelling me forward was the desire for it all to be over.

And then I was afraid of people.

Those who did *not* frighten me as a child (until I grew to know them better) could be described as follows:

- Self-aware, especially of one's physical body in relationship to another's. These people maintained a certain distance for a handshake. They showed grace and propriety, were neither overly loud or especially quiet, were mild tempered, not given to argue, act hastily, or be pushy.

- Unimposing. They didn't tease, pry, show unadulterated affection, or invade one's privacy. They never told me how I should think.

- Clean. It didn't matter to me what the person wore or even what they looked like, but evidence of self-care, or the lack thereof, spoke volumes to me.

- Not needy. It was all I could do as a child to take care of myself. My own needs and wants were voluminous, and I worked them in my mind like worry beads, endlessly. I had no room for anything else.

It just occurred to me that I have described my husband. He is the perfect partner for me.

My fear of people undoubtedly stemmed from my expectations of them. I was not carefree; I could not just "go with the flow." I needed to know what people might be like or how events might unfold before I encountered them. I needed a preview so I could consider all angles in advance. This was not your garden-variety social anxiety but something else. It had to do with a small child's need to control her environment, to know her place and the place of others. I had such tightly held boundaries that when crossed, I was driven to violently self-protective fits.

My mother has always claimed I was "keeper of The Book of Rules" as a child. I would become testy if people did not act the way I thought they were supposed to act. I would generally turn inward to mull over my level of discomfort and think about ways to get away from them. If I was pressed too far, however, I would let the whole world know. My stern little body could be a force to be reckoned with, and my tantrums were frightening enough for everyone to stop what they were otherwise doing and come watch me stomp in rage and throw myself on the floor. It was at those times that my family would notice me, perhaps for the first time in several days or weeks. I was a quiet, self-possessed child otherwise, with my nose in a book or helping my mother in the kitchen. I rarely ventured outside, preferring made-up games of having Queen Elizabeth and Princess Margaret for tea, or coloring steadfastly in countless coloring books until my rainbow of markers ran dry.

Growing up, I had no great harm come to me, sandwiched between my much louder and vibrant brother and sister, reared by loving and liberal parents. I do know, however, that my early fear of people is one reason I would be so deeply tested by my experience working at Stratford.

By the time I became a young woman, I had traveled to and

lived in several foreign countries, studied and read enough history, literature, science, psychology, and religion to have overcome my fear of strangers and of people who were different from me. But the discomforts of our childhood shape us silently and urgently toward adulthood, leaving a dusty trail of footprints from our past. Education and open-mindedness instilled from birth and increasing maturity counteracted the naïve, safety-seeking attitudes of my youth that nevertheless left their marks.

Once my parents had decided to go east to run the halfway house, we took several weeks driving to Cambridge, heading north first so we could camp along the way in Canada. I recall the long hours in the warm car wedged between my siblings, our hands sticky from dried fruit and nuts, Cheetos, and juice. My mother, a former kindergarten teacher, had devised several games to keep us entertained. I Spy petered out after five or six rounds, though, and after that I was in and out of fuzzy dreams, my chin slumped on my chest.

At the border between Washington and Canada, the man in a gray-green uniform waved my father over to the side. My mother clucked under her breath, and my father gently put a hand on her knee. The war in Vietnam was not yet over. As a teacher, married with three children, my father had been excused from the draft. But who knows what was going through his mind?

All five of us were asked to get out of the car, which I hardly minded. I stretched my chubby legs and shook my head until my braids smacked my face and I was momentarily, blissfully

dizzy. We sat inside an air-conditioned room on mustard yellow chairs. My feet swung back and forth over the floor. A
woman with the tallest head of blond hair I had ever seen sat
behind a glass partition with a small opening. I was fascinated by her hair, teased up into something that looked like a
soft-serve ice cream cone frozen by shiny spray that reflected
the light from a side window. Not a lock was out of place.
She took some paperwork from my mother, who glared at
her. The woman seemed unconcerned, which was not how
people usually responded to my mother. I examined her a
bit more closely, noting her long red nails, her substantial
bosom holding up her name badge. "Madge," it read.

Madge came out from behind her desk, emerging through
a door I had not noticed until she stepped through it. She
must have been sitting on a tall stool, because I expected her
to tower over everything in the room, a blond, red-nailed,
busty giant. She wore sturdy desert boots and straight chino
pants with a hefty belt, but she couldn't have been more than
five feet two. She looked at my sister, who was sucking a stale
lollipop discovered in a jar by the front door, and then at my
brother, standing by the chair next to mine, seemingly reading but actually shredding a *Time* magazine he had grabbed
from the coffee table in the waiting room. Last, she looked at
me, locking on to my blue eyes with her own.

I could feel my mother silently daring the woman to say
whatever she had planned to say. A wall clock ticked off the
seconds as Madge appraised me with a girlish sparkle in her
eyes. Mom stood a bit to the side, behind her, her lips pursed,

one hand pressed against her hip. My father leaned against a post nearby, his fingers tapping quietly at the Camels in his left breast pocket. He looked sleepy after all those hours behind the wheel.

"Well, hello, sweetheart." Madge smiled down at me, her red-lipped mouth stretching open to reveal straight, slightly stained teeth.

"Hi," I said.

"Is this your sister?" She nodded over to Caitlin, who had been born with incredibly black and thick eyebrows, which furrowed slightly under Madge's scrutiny. Caitlin pulled the lollipop out of her mouth with a quick suction sound.

"Yes," I said. "My sister, Caitlin."

Madge nodded as if that was clearly the right answer. What a stupid question! I wondered if Madge was a little off, or missing a few screws, as my father would say. Madge then looked at my brother, who turned away from his magazine shredding and put his hand on her leg to steady himself. He smiled at her, the smile that had always impelled me to get on a chair and climb into his crib to snuggle next to him, while I read him a story.

"And who is this?" Madge asked. Her leg was sturdy, and Josh wrapped his other arm around it like a tree. My mother, I could see, could hardly contain herself. She looked like a lioness about to pounce. My father, more alert now, appeared to be on the verge of laughing.

"My little brother, Josh," I answered her sternly. I jumped off the chair and pulled his small brown hands from her leg and turned him toward me, picking him up briefly off the floor against his mild protests. I had never been overly protective of my brother; he had not seemed to need my protection. But there was something unkind I sensed in Madge's appraisal of him. There was something fishy, too, about why my family had been pulled aside while cars in front of us and cars behind us had been waved on through.

Josh, whose skin was the color of coffee mixed with milk, had been adopted at two weeks old. Maybe Madge didn't understand how Josh could be my brother. But the paperwork my parents gave her was the paperwork that tied Josh to us forever. And my answer satisfied Madge. Josh was my brother. We had not stolen him.

We used the restroom while my father smoked a cigarette outside. Mom bought us sugary sodas in ice-cold glass bottles from the vending machine next to the building. We all piled back into the Toyota, the afternoon sun wrapping us up in our own private thoughts as we drove on.

4

WELCOME TO CHAOS

My interview at Stratford had taken place in September, and I was offered the job a couple of weeks later, after Wendy had put in a battle to get me the salary I requested.

"You have a master's degree, after all!" She yelled into the phone with the good news. "If they want to attract people of your caliber, they need to pay for it." She was so proud of the number, though I yearned to be able to negotiate further, even to refuse. It was barely half the salary I had taken in my last year of employment at Textron Financial. I grimaced, looking out my front window at the cul-de-sac. A neighbor boy was throwing a basketball at the neighborhood hoop. The ball hit the board several times, once landing in the prickly ivy behind it. He gamely kept shooting, and finally it went in the net.

"I'm thrilled to accept your offer," I told her. "I can't wait to start!" I bit my lip hard with my false enthusiasm.

"Super! Amazing! We can't wait to have you there! You are going to do fabulous things!" Wendy's glee embraced me like an older sister's hug. "Now, here's the thing. As you know, they are remodeling Stratford. It's on a construction schedule, and I am sure you know things don't always go as planned. They are a couple weeks behind right now."

I felt the old panic creeping into my veins as I listened to her. Of course they were remodeling. I had witnessed the early stages of the construction work at my first and only interview, which ended up being a panel session. There were seven people there to meet me, their faces all smiling and hopeful, seated around a table in a room with a sheet of plastic hanging from the doorway. My ten-year-old self cringed while my forty-two-year-old self kept control.

"So when did you think I might start?" I asked cautiously.

"My thought was," mused Wendy, "let's go ahead and say November 1, and we'll try and be flexible about it." I was to learn that "flexible" was one of Wendy's favorite words. She used it like one might lean on one's vice—smoking, drinking, binge television show watching. She had me in a corner, with visions of my first paycheck arriving just before my severance had gone to zero, before my family's COBRA insurance— up until that point covered under President Obama's ARRA plan—became my bill to pay.

I swallowed my disappointment and did my best to volley back her enthusiasm. "Sounds great!" Four more weeks loomed in front of me like an open plain, nothing but cloudy skies as far as the eye could see.

On the morning of my first day at ElderHome in Stratford, I peered into my closet and thumbed through suits, dresses, slacks, and sweaters. It was unseasonably warm for the beginning of November. The morning sun was streaming through the dark red leaves of the tree in the neighbor's yard. I chose carefully, wanting to make a good impression with the numerous people I expected to be introduced to throughout the day. Wendy had promised a long lineup, as if I were at a coming-out reception, a nervous and young girl in her flouncy dress and white gloves. I decided to dress the part and chose a royal blue dress with cap sleeves and a fitted waist that hid my large calves and highlighted my eyes. I topped it off with a black cardigan and pulled out some black leather pumps.

Sweaters had become as frequent an accessory as my handbag, along with gloves, both fingerless and full, as I entered my fourth decade. Scleroderma, the autoimmune disorder that I had been diagnosed with in my early thirties, manifested itself in part as Raynaud's. Throughout the day if there was any notable drop in temperature, the blood flow to my hands and feet would slow, leaving my fingertips bluish purple and swollen.

As I walked out of the house, Jay gave me one of his airtight hugs that always left me breathless. "You've got this," he said, his hand warm on my lower back.

Something wrenched at me as I pulled out of our drive and out onto the street. Tears welled into my eyes, and I wiped them away quickly. A storm of thoughts brewed in my mind. I could not define what I was feeling; it was all so mixed up. I was thinking about my children and the time I had gotten to spend with them those past seven months. It was the only time I had been able to be a stay-at-home mom since I returned to work after a standard three months' maternity leave for each child. The sense of having lost something in those intervening years was palpable. The kids were both so independent and brave. They did not rely on me for help and comfort like some children did with their mothers. If they fell and scraped their elbow, they found the Neosporin and Band-Aids in the hall closet and carefully applied them on their own. If they woke before I did on the weekends, they made their own eggs and waffles and poured juice into a glass without spilling. They rarely asked for help with their homework; they knew how numbers and emails consumed my day and had learned to let me unwind by cooking dinner, while they sat on a barstool and answered my questions about school, friends, and soccer.

I had carefully chosen the other adults who had tended to them when I was not there, and they were never perfect; I simply trained myself to not wonder what was going on all day long. Otherwise the wondering would turn to a grief that is unlike anything else, a heart-pounding sense of loss.

It had never been easy. I would drop the kids off at day care or school and watch their little backs covered in puffy coats and packs of books. When I picked them up at the end of the workday, they looked so small, hardy but worn, and my heart would break with love and longing for them and the full days of their growing that I had missed.

As I drove, I was also thinking about Textron, where I had worked from before their births and into their early childhood, and where I had grown up myself as a businessperson. Textron was family, a place with a regular hum, a constant revolve, like Earth circling the sun. It was a place where I learned about the corporate world, where I developed skills in credit and risk management that I could exercise in my sleep today. Those of us who worked there thought it would last forever. It didn't.

When Textron shut down our office in Lake Oswego, it was like a death in the family.

This was where we had all shown up with our first set of work clothes, sensible but sassy shoes, our leftover dinners tucked in our tote bags to microwave at lunch. This was where we gossiped between cubicles, surfed the internet when it was new and forbidden, migrated in small groups to nearby restaurants for a beer or glass of wine after hours. This was where we talked about our weekend dates, about moving in together, engagements, and wedding plans. Where we shared news of our first pregnancies, car accidents, home-buying experiences, health problems, tropical vacations, more babies, and divorces, and where we had our company Christmas parties, election debates, and social faux pas.

Those of us who joined the company in the mid-1990s had formed a tight bond. We put new employees through a silent hazing, determined who told inappropriate jokes, who was the office flirt or curmudgeon, and who harbored secrets, such as porn addiction, alcoholism, or spousal abuse. We leaned on each other and teased each other relentlessly. We talked about everything from the inane (granny underwear vs. sexy thongs, best tuna casserole recipe, or marinade for flank steak) to the heartbreaking (a seventh miscarriage, a dad who deserted the family, putting one's mother in an assisted living facility).

We had lived through harrowing times together at Textron, especially on the day we all heard of two airplanes crashing into the twin towers in New York. Silence filled the room, and at first none of us could bear to look at each other. The first few minutes it was as if a fire alarm had sounded and then abruptly ended. And there we stood, frozen in place, instead of piling down the exterior stairs to the parking lot below.

Time seemed to stop. There was the sound of birds outside the office windows, a soft mist of rain on the panes. Down the hall, a toilet flushed. We turned on the two televisions in the office and set them up in different conference rooms. People wandered in and out like patients waiting in the ER holding their heads and arms, listening for their name to be called.

The news unfolded painfully, like the slow drip of melting snow. Some of us slumped at desks, clicking on various internet sites, tapping on cell phones as we remembered yet another family member or friend to call. *Are you okay? I'm okay. The kids are okay. Did you know anyone there? Have you heard from Uncle Doug/cousin Maria/Bev's partner, Del?*

No one was working. At some point our president, Dave, trudged around the perimeter of the office, stopping to talk quietly to an employee here and there. He had never talked quietly before.

In 2008, when we were told the office would be closed and the company shut down in anticipation of the looming Great Recession, you might as well have told us our house would be burned down with all of us in it. It seemed like 9/11 all over again.

I would often revisit Textron in my mind during my time at Stratford and for years after. There was nothing that compared to those years, nothing at all. I remembered the uncomfortable and upsetting times, but they didn't matter to me. All I wanted to do was hold on to my personal rendition of the past like a child savoring an ice cream cone one lick at a time.

Despite my daydreaming, my car seemed to know where it was going, and I was powerless to stop its forward momentum. I bit my lips, a bad habit that would lead to an endless cycle of chapping, ChapStick, and more lip biting. I remembered the first word I told myself in the waiting room at Stratford the day I met Karen and Miss Lonnie: *cheerful*. I was certainly not cheerful by nature. In repose, my mouth rested in a serious, testy line, and my general posture was somewhat tense and could be read as standoffish. I had tried tirelessly over the years to counteract that impression, even though I suspected it worked in my favor as both a mother and a manager.

At Stratford, I was entering a world where taking care of people in need was the objective and the mission. I hoped that I had been hired more for my management skills than my love for people. I don't, in general, love people. I am cautious, selective. I love the small group of people I have chosen to love and who love me back, but an introvert can only handle so much intimacy. It overwhelms us to the point of senselessness. A crowded room, the tumult of too many personal odors and voices, the ridiculous certainty that there's no way out, the dread of making small talk—it wears an introvert down to the point of utter exhaustion.

But my mother had raised me to think positively! Surely the greatest burden of caregiving at Stratford would be borne by others. I had been hired to manage the operations of the building and oversee the medical clinic. My role was to right the ship, for the facility had been losing more than a million dollars a year. I would apply all that I knew to turning it around financially, to creating a positive cash flow while keeping the staff happy and motivated.

Sure, there would be some challenges. The facility housed a broad spectrum of men and women from all walks of life. I knew the residents had health problems, thanks to bad luck, hard times, and a lifetime of poor choices. That's why they qualified for residency at Stratford. In order to be able to live at an ElderHome facility, you had to have health problems, be on Medicaid, and have very little income, under a particular state dictated threshold. Still, luck now seemed to be on their side. They had been accepted into the building, where all their needs could be met. They had people to care for them, a roof over their head, medicine for when their pain was high and their thoughts low. I would ensure that the framework for that—the services, the safety, the socialization—stayed consistent and available. I had my master's degree tucked into my back pocket like a map to orient me. All my positivity wheels were spinning, spinning every negative thought into something malleable and fixable!

It's hard now not to laugh at my incredible naïveté, but trust me, within a matter of weeks, I was not laughing.

5

THE BOOK OF RULES

As I've noted, my mother often referred to me as the keeper of The Book of Rules growing up. The Rules were what kept me safe and reassured me in countless ways that life was predictable. When it was not, I became uncomfortable, my nerves on edge.

Living at the halfway house in Cambridge—a rambling Victorian three stories tall, with seven or eight bedrooms—tested my developing understanding of The Rules. Everyone who lived in the house had longish hair, sharp shoulder blades, drooping jeans, and bohemian blouses embroidered and beaded with wolves, rainbows, and stardust. An aura of lethargy permeated the common spaces.

I spent most of my time inside, and when tired of playing with my Barbie dolls or picture books I would get up to wander the house, passing by open bedroom doors where people in various stages of undress and sleep lay on futons and bare mattresses or sat puffing on cigarettes. The breeze from the open windows would blow the smoke back into the hall. They would smile and beckon to me, and if I came to sit with them, they'd run their fingers through my fine hair. Some people played the guitar, while others sang sorrowful songs about war, flowers, and freedom.

They all seemed lost in their own way. Some had never stopped taking drugs, and most smoked weed. My parents really didn't monitor them closely. It was a free-spirited world, everything tinted a golden hue. I was not frightened by my housemates; I believe I was intrigued. I could breathe easily around these people who were high on drugs; their needs were muted, their claws pulled in.

But all was not what it seemed. Underneath the surface was the tumult that had brought the young people to this house—an inability to function in mainstream society; mental illness; angry, controlling parents; eating disorders; suicide attempts; a desire to numb it all with drugs and alcohol. The house reflected their complete disregard for convention. Its contents were beat up. Filth from bare feet and unwashed clothing accumulated on the floors. Spaghetti pots were piled in the kitchen sink, and oil leaked from motorbikes and Volkswagen vans parked out by the curb.

One day Greg, one of the housemates, gave each of us children a ride on his motorcycle around the block. Caitlin and Josh rode together gleefully, Caitlin using one hand to hold Josh around his waist and the other to grip Greg's leather-vested back. I was determined to take my turn too. Someone hoisted me up behind Greg, whose girlfriend's helmet more than covered my small head, while my short three-year-old legs sweated on the leather seat.

It was just one loop around the block, but I still remember how my little heart felt, as if it flew out of my chest and smashed on the pavement. My eyes were screwed shut the entire five-minute ride. When we returned, Ian, another housemate, pulled me off the bike with his large hands, the same hands I held on to when he walked me to preschool weekday mornings. I was in my late twenties before I could get on a motorcycle again.

Ian was a graduate student, writing his psychology dissertation on my family. In his final draft, he observed that in the context of my family, I was raising myself.

A year after we arrived in Cambridge, the halfway house burned down. On the night of the fire, my mother woke each of us by banging pots and pans, her white cotton nightgown flying out behind her as she rushed around the two rooms the five of us shared.

"Choose your two favorite things and follow me!" Her eyes were snapping. Josh, Caitlin, and I did as we were told. My father was nowhere to be seen. Days later I discovered he had been in the backyard, throwing household items into the stand-up pool in an effort to save them. There would be no more swimming that summer.

By 2 a.m. we were sitting on the steps of the house across the street, watching the halfway house burn down. The flames had started in the attic, my father told us later, where someone fell asleep while smoking pot. The neighbor brought out some blankets, and we curled into them as the sirens of the firetrucks drew nearer. The neighbor looked at the three of us kids and then at my mother.

"Who is this child?" she asked, pointing at me. I ignored her. I had never seen her either.

"That's my middle daughter, Erin," my mother answered, an eyebrow raised. The woman nodded, and we were all silent again. Wasn't there some rule about knowing your neighbors? I wondered.

Not long after that, we returned to Portland, and I continued to develop my understanding of The Rules. These ran the gamut of what time one should go to bed at what age and to how to tie your shoelaces to how to drink tea (straight: no sugar, no lemon, and most certainly no cream) and the way you were supposed to talk to people (no harping, no shouting, no meanness). If I saw others breaking The Rules, I would find a creative way to advise them of their error. Usually the person would just scoff at me or, worse, laugh at my presumption.

When it came to rule enforcement, my brother took the path of increasing or doubling up on whatever rule he had broken, just to mock and frustrate me. If he was singing the same song over and over on a long car ride, I would point out that I couldn't hear my own thoughts. He would just crunch closer to me and increase both the volume and the tempo of his song. If there were two cookies left on a plate, he would eat one, and, when I remarked it was polite to ask if anyone else cared for one, he would promptly snatch up the remaining cookie, pile it on top of the half-eaten one in his mouth, and spew crumbs as he stared me down, grinning. My father would silently laugh along with him, while my sister chewed her nails (food was of zero interest to her, ever), and my mother slapped him lightly with an "oh, Josh." Then she'd let me know there was plenty of *fruit* in the house if I was still hungry.

The Rules covered when it was okay to start smoking cigarettes (my friend Hallie and I began with a pack of Winstons in a dugout near our schoolyard when we were both ten) and when to drink beer in public. The rule for that was age fourteen, at the senior graduation party, though my father, who firmly believed milk was poison to children after age twelve and they should switch to beer instead, had offered it to me much earlier. Actually that was a joke that my father loved to tell houseguests when offering *them* a beer, but most of my parents' friends never questioned it, since the general view was that my parents had done a fine job of raising us to that point. My parents *did* believe in removing any mystery around alcohol so that my siblings and I would not have a need to chase after it like something forbidden.

The Rules included when it was practical and appropriate to start using four-letter words. I think my use of foul language started around age twelve. Hallie and I tested out "fuck," "shit," and "asshole" on each other. I preferred "fuck" and used it indiscriminately with my closest friends, while Hallie preferred "asshole." Everyone was an asshole to Hallie, and she would say it with a coy smile while she sucked in the smoke from a Marlboro Light. (We had decided Marlboros tasted the best after trying several brands of cigarettes and clove cigarettes since our first puff of Winstons.)

We both agreed that words that demeaned women—
"cunt," "bitch," and "pussy," to list a few—had no place
in our swearing vocabulary. "Cunt" especially was offensive
to us, and if we overheard anyone, especially a boy, using
the word we'd threaten to cut off their "dicks." As you can
see, The Rules only went one way. We most certainly could
use swear words that were offensive to men (though notably
there are few).

I had strong rules about the attitudes men should display
toward women. I recall a very tall middle school teacher
with brown eyes, glasses, and a narrow black beard tow-
ering over me across the table in an empty classroom, his
long arms reaching for my hands, as I shrunk back against
the metal chair.

"Why are you so uncomfortable with me, Erin?" he
asked after my rejection. What adult asks that of a thirteen-year-old girl, feeling awkward within all her newly
active hormones and wearing 501 shrink-to-fit Levi's over
her expanding hips?

I also remember being furious at seeing a dear childhood
friend seated on the lap of an older family acquaintance long
after a party had ended and the other adults had gone to bed.

And one day, when I was around ten, waiting for the bus
after my ballet class, I noticed a man smoking a cigarette and
ogling the woman next to him, his self-pride evident by the
spread of his legs, just so, on the sidewalk and the way he
spoke to her. I did not at all like the way he put his hands on
her, as if she were something he owned outright.

Somewhere in the back of my mind I had a rule about when one should lose their virginity. To me that was something you should just get out of the way, a chore like cleaning out the garage or organizing your taxes, regardless of whether you were in love. I was sure that this would make love easier to approach and enjoy when it really mattered, with a person you were passionate about. Sixteen seemed about the right age, so I was appalled when I'd hear of a friend doing it at fourteen and curious when I met women who were in their late twenties and still had their hymen intact.

I was convinced my own hymen had been ruptured by an extremely painful hard landing on the bar of my men's bike when I was cycling in Europe on a student trip at age thirteen. Based on that experience and the subsequent bleeding and bruising, I figured I was halfway through the woods for my first time. I didn't conform to the sixteen-year-old age goal. As it turned out, I didn't get my chance until a few years later.

The Book of Rules was, of course, grounded in a certain philosophy I had as a young girl for living a happy and prosperous life. I have always believed that propriety and good manners were its foundation, and as I matured, I put these beliefs to the test by deploying various rules in whatever manner suited me. I wasn't aware of the hypocrisy of changing The Rules along the way, until I was old enough to know better.

Sound and practical advice were added to the good manners that I thought everyone should live by. Emily Post and Dear Abby were two of my go-to experts, as were nineteenth-century British novelists and a few literary types who wrote before World War II. By my estimation, most good manners in the United States were lost after World War II. Maybe it had something to do with television, or maybe it was the horrifying diet (fast, greasy, heavy in dairy and corn, sopping sweet) that became popular in the 1950s and that set Americans on a path of obesity and moodiness.

As a keeper of The Book of Rules, you expect the best from people until they prove you otherwise. This belief that all people are born wanting to naturally follow certain rules is not a new idea and has been propounded by great philosophers such as Socrates, Confucius, and Rousseau. The problem is that philosophy is not science, and, in fact, people do not always behave well, me included. Anyone who works with the public knows this. Teachers, for example, struggle to maintain their composure when little Astrid, for the third time in a semester, sticks her gum under another student's chair or throws spit wads at the ceiling. Police officers pull over speeding drivers only to notice the two children asleep in the back, no seat belts fastened around their small waists. Coffeeshop baristas who fail to get someone's order done right face both an angry, caffeine-hungry customer and the aggrieved and impatient queue of other patrons who are forced to wait while the barista hurriedly fixes the mistake.

Coming from the field of financial services, I had a specific kind of customer, and our interactions could be narrowed down to a very small chapter in The Book of Rules. Our relationship was simple: The customer needed financing from my company to acquire goods, build things, expand their operations, and so forth, and I was the person who could make that financing available to them. When someone wants something from you under these circumstances, even if they are paying for it, they are usually friendly, accommodating, and earnest. Obviously they want you to say yes to them. They want you to like their company and to agree that giving them money is a great idea. And when you need to find out more about the company to reach this decision, you do so in a way that gains their trust, pleases them, and assures them they've made a good choice working with you and your company.

These exchanges sound like a game, but they are more like an art, a painting that you work on together. When it's all done, you get to toast the way it turned out, wine glasses clinking. Sometimes we would celebrate with a fine dinner; other times we would send a glass "tombstone" etched with our name and the customer's and noting the millions we provided and what it was for. I could count on one hand the number of times a customer behaved badly or complained, the times someone ran off with our collateral (usually trucks), stole our money (collected it from their own customer who was supposed to pay us instead), or simply disappeared, leaving us with just a social security number and thousands of dollars in debt. The truth was, for the most part I had worked with decent folk, looking to do well, following The Rules. Despite my inclination to scrutinize and question people's character and their motives, I never really questioned the goals of my customers in the financial world.

My relationship with them put Gunnar's favorite chicken fingers on the table and Camille's soccer cleats in her backpack. My paychecks were generous.

When I came to work at Stratford, I assumed that my "customers" might be fusty, down on their luck, unwell, and old, but that The Rules would still apply. I was due for an awakening.

6

COMING AND GOING

That first day I walked into Stratford I was assailed by the smell of sheetrock and dust. The main entry of the facility had the feel of a busy subway station, except there were no trains, and no one was really going anywhere. Staff and visitors conversed; residents swallowed pills, sat, shouted, sang, ate, drank coffee, got their blood pressure checked, read the paper, and generally gazed into the middle distance.

Unlike the day of my interview, there was a different woman at the front desk. Her name was Jewell, who turned out to be a close friend, almost a twin by their striking similarities, of Jeannine, the woman who worked the evening shift. Jewell was maybe nineteen, had serious mahogany eyes, and was constantly moving, slowly and steadily, much like a sternwheeler. My office was located behind her desk, and she directed me there, past the stack of cardboard boxes (medical and other supplies) and rubber-banded piles of mail that she had not yet sorted.

I took quick stock of the miscellany that flowed from

under the desk and along the wall, stopping just at the door into my office. The assortment of goods was astonishing: Costco-size pretzel bags; a container of red licorice; lost-and-found items such as one yellow rainboot, a chestnut brown woman's wig, a hand-knit beret, and a dream catcher. Boxes of paperwork (likely containing information not compliant with HIPAA) gathered dust. Rounding out the mix were party supplies, Christmas ornaments, sheet music, a dog's water dish, and dirty plates from the kitchen with a glaze of brown gravy drying under a fork.

The office had a heavy metal door that closed soundly behind you, and a thick glass window that revealed staff mailboxes over a counter. To the right was my inner office, containing a small round table with two chairs, a grimy maple-colored desk, a metal file cabinet, and a multipaned window overlooking the sidewalk next to the relatively quiet side street. This room would become both my sanctuary and my prison cell over the next eighteen months as hundreds of people came through it during the workweek. Depending on the meetings (brief, lengthy, unexpected, scheduled, worrisome, shocking, delusional, hopeful, and otherwise), I would either feel like a trapped animal or a barely effective manager.

What my new job was really like dawned on me within the first three weeks. The chaotic nature of an assisted living facility is one thing, but Stratford was in a world of its own. The hospital system of which ElderHome was a division had gone outside their historical business model and acquired the building and taken over the management of Stratford from a

Detroit operator who had let the facility go into decline and paid little attention to who moved in. The ElderHome model specified that a resident had to be older than fifty-five, on Medicaid, and require some sort of services. The services fell under the category of ADLs—that is, activities of daily living, such as eating, dressing, and taking medication.

When ElderHome came in, they cleaned up the five-story, 130-apartment building physically with a remodel and by starting to open a medical clinic on-site. But they were not able to "clean up" the building in terms of population demographics. As a result, some residents met only two out of three of the criteria. For example, a number of people were under fifty-five, in some cases significantly younger.

There were other differences. Stratford had become a destination for several generations of families in the neighborhood. These families might send Grandma Nell, then Aunt Pearl, then cousin Hank who moved out here from Texas and rapidly declined, then their neighbor's son Johnny who was never quite right. All had been accepted and were catered to by staff who had also worked there for a long time and who were often related in some fashion to the residents. Favoritism and nepotism abounded.

Stratford also had the reputation as the home of last resort for people with behavioral issues who had been kicked out of other facilities. There was angry Liza who had scores of health problems stemming from her years of heroin abuse and prostitution. Lyle, the repeat sex offender, who everyone hoped was now too old to continue his past activities.

Jackson, the quiet bipolar man who shuffled along from meals to arts and crafts hour but never seemed to require services of any kind until the day he pulled a screwdriver out of his right pocket and stabbed another resident in the arm.

They were among the people discussed at regular meetings with my peers, who managed other assisted living facilities with more familiar characteristics: soft-spoken older adults with table manners, minor complaints, and easily addressed needs. Places where the daily events included napping, subdued music in the background, and folks engaged in card games with little contention or side talk.

I would share updates about Stratford, and the group would nod in unison. With compassionate smiles on their faces, they would offer suggestions on how to address Mr. Silver's behavioral issues at mealtime, or Mrs. Knapp's kleptomania. I would feel warmed by their attention, reassured, and spitting mad all at once. I wanted to clobber them, too, since I felt helpless in the face of their empathy, which I only partially trusted. I assumed there was something wrong with me, because how could all of them have been doing this work for so long and still walk around as though nothing was amiss?

"Ahh, yes, Stratford," one of the more supportive operations managers would say, shaking her head wisely. "In part, it's the population you have. We can't just kick them out, so we must see the nature of Stratford evolve with attrition."

Attrition, it seemed, would come after violence allowed us to remove a person from the facility (the process was still painfully drawn out) or upon the death of the resident. On rare occasions someone would decide Stratford just wasn't for them and ask to move. The process for finding a new place for them to live was also an arduous task. There were multiple phone calls and lots of paperwork on my part to arrange visits and rides for the visits and to provide personal health information to administrators of the other potential housing sites.

Other times the resident might just disappear. If the person's needs were minimal and no one spoke up, their absence could go unnoticed. At some point, another resident would say they hadn't seen so-and-so in the dining room for a couple of days. We would knock on so-and-so's door and eventually do a "wellness check" if we got no answer. That meant we'd go in search of Rhonda, the intake specialist, who had the master key, and with a nurse in front and me behind, we would gently nudge open the door. Anything might be found there.

There was the occasional scene where an ambulance was required. This was always unexpected because those in need of care—the sick, the dying, the depressed, those with regular medication and monitoring—would have never been missed by routine checks and medication assistance. It was the small flock of more independent people who either gave up, gave in, or moved on. Their needs may have been as great, if not *more* devastating than those who were under doctor's orders or required assistance, but they had either rejected the notion of help or been found to not qualify for it. They just fell through the cracks.

As I discovered, Stratford resembled a long-running soap opera. Anything that could happen to a person happened at Stratford. It had once been unfathomable to me how the writers for *General Hospital* and *Days of Our Lives* kept coming up with new material year after year. Not anymore.

Most times on a wellness check, we'd walk into an ice-cold or feverishly hot room (the AC or the heat had been left on) with a table lamp still lit, the toilet seat up, and the blanket on the bed tossed aside. After finding the resident gone, we would call their "primary contact," if they had one. We didn't spend too much time looking for the person; that was the family's or friend's affair, and where would we have looked? A major bus line stopped right in front of the building, and the center of Portland was only blocks away. You could hear the MAX light rail in the distance, and Amtrak, leading to Seattle, Boise, and beyond, was a mere mile or two down the road at the end of the Burnside Bridge.

The other residents would pass along tales about the disappearance: "Marvin told us he had a girlfriend waiting for him in Baton Rouge." Or "Bevvy's granddaughter was stealing from her. She probably went to stay with her sister who lives in a motor-home park down at Coos Bay." Or they'd muse about more mystical or dire outcomes. "Look, there was something kooky going on with that woman Charlotte. You saw all the crystals and incense in her room, no? Maybe she transformed herself into a rainbow, and that's her laughing at you right now." Or "Perry was up to no good. I told him once if I told him twice to not hang with those low-down fools he played poker with. I am sure he's deep in the river now with a concrete block tied to his feet." These sorts of stories were usually traded at the front desk after dark, when Jewell's counterpart, Jeannine, had taken up her post.

"Shh, shh, Mr. Tandy," Jeannine would say, flicking her long fingernails in the speaker's direction. "Don't speak so mean about things you don't know about."

We did notify the police, who would come in to take a missing person's report. The police were familiar with Stratford and would stroll in laconically, stifle a yawn, dust off their notepads, and ask a few perfunctory questions. Some residents seemed drawn to the presence of the law like mosquitos to blood and would buzz about the entryway but not look the officers directly in the eye. Others would scatter, going out the side or back doors or up the elevators to their rooms. The police never requested a photo before they left. My sense was they wanted only a general description in the event they discovered a body somewhere behind a dumpster or along the banks of the Willamette and needed a quick close to the case.

Sometimes after a week the missing would wander back in reeking of alcohol, disheveled and sleepy-eyed. Other times they would be returned by a relative who had taken them to an Indian reservation to gamble for a few days. We got only shrugs when we reminded them of our in-and-out procedures. There was a procedure for everything, but some residents still treated the building like a normal apartment building, where you could remain anonymous, set your own schedule, and bring in whomever you wanted. This led to a score of problems, and our night manager's phone would ring at 2:30 a.m., police would be called about rowdiness, locks would be changed, and grievances would be logged. It was a wonder anyone ever slept.

I personally escorted one resident's "girlfriend" out on several occasions. Once she discovered there were several men in the building with enough cash to pay for her services, she snuck in as often as possible. One night I caught her arriving at midnight when I was on call. Her skirt was so short and her heels so high she tottered like a flamingo and swung her gold purse about like a wing flapping. Her eyes were weighed down by huge fake eyelashes, and her lipstick was a glowing burgundy. Her short top revealed a spray of tattoos across her belly. I wanted both to yell at her and put her to bed in nice clean sheets so she could sleep with no one touching her, no one pulling her hair or gripping her by the hips. Instead, when I tried to put my hand on her arm, she jerked away like a skittish colt.

"Don't touch me! I was just leavin'!" She waved me off. Surprisingly she smelled of gardenias, and her eyes were clear and bright, but resentful that I had cut into her profits for the night.

"Bye, Allan!" she yelled down the hall. "I'll see you later!" And with one last hassled glance at me over her shoulder, she was gone.

For those who had truly disappeared from Stratford, we'd wait the allotted amount of time and then clean out their rooms. Residents lined up eagerly to see if there was any-thing worth taking.

On the rarest of occasions, a generous family member or friend would offer a resident a room in their own home or whisk them off to Florida for a quick trip. Sometimes these people were sent back, showing up in a taxi at the front door, a clammy note gripped in their hand, with a battered suitcase, their meds off track, their hair unwashed. The sight of them shuffling in like someone who doesn't want to be noticed made my heart bend with sorrow.

Emotions quickly began to overwhelm me. Over the next year, I would cry in my parked car in the mornings before slowly gathering myself together and willing my body to walk into the building for yet another day. As time went on, I would cry in my office, mostly in the afternoons, even though I knew that my door could be blasted open at any moment by anyone who felt it was important to talk to the operations manager that very second, no appointment required. I never knew I was capable of so many tears. I was crying for all of us.

It wasn't long before every interaction at Stratford started to feel like an internal bruise, the kind you discover weeks after a car accident. But like a senseless bird flying repeatedly into a plate-glass window, I kept showing up every day.

7

REMODELING

After we came back to Portland from Cambridge, my parents rented a shotgun apartment on the second floor of a three-story Art Deco building in the northwest part of town. The apartment was technically a one bedroom but also had an "office"—a room with two large sliding doors off the living room that was more likely intended for formal dining—and an enclosed sunporch. Depending on the season, my sister and I would sleep in bunk beds on the sunporch or in a queen bed in the bedroom, where my brother had a small cot. My parents slept in the office.

The building was encumbered with various arthropods and insects, including termites, cockroaches, and mealy bugs. My mother became an expert at periodically eliminating them through various spontaneous methods, but they always returned, like children coming home from summer camp, sunburned head to toe and having grown a couple of inches.

In fact, all sorts of creatures lived among us in abundance. My mother developed an interest in turtles and acquired three, which were called Flat Pat, Red, and Gandalf. For entertainment my mother would order a turtle "race," and we would line up all three of them on the living room carpet, facing toward the kitchen. My siblings and I would get to choose our racer for the day, and if our turtle managed to go the farthest toward the kitchen, we'd win the prize. The prize could be anything from a dollar or being first in line for dinner to a trip to the corner store for a candy bar. The turtles, being turtles, would tuck their feet and heads in and refuse to move, or they might take a few steps to the right and then freeze, their beady eyes darting all about, or they'd move as fast as they could for about a yard and then turn around.

We also had a boa constrictor named Basil. At feeding time my father would drop one tiny mouse into his cage. Basil would play with his food a while before opening his incongruously large jaws and swallowing it whole. I would hide in the bedroom on feeding days.

Sometime after we got Basil, we acquired a white rat with watery pink eyes. My brother named him after my father—Sam. Sam ate so voraciously he bloomed into a dirty, round, slothful thing that rarely moved. Josh was disappointed that Sam didn't do much but stare at us from his cage. We also had guinea pigs, and the guinea pigs gave birth to more guinea pigs, but most of them didn't live more than a few days. My mother would wrap the babies up in a brown paper bag and put the bag in the trash bin behind the building. I was routinely disturbed to the point of tears by this lack of ceremony. I vividly recall trying to tear one of the little body bags from my mother's hands as she folded it over perfunctorily in the kitchen.

There was a lot of drama created by this veritable zoo on NW Northrup Street. My mother was often exasperated by us children during this time, and on several occasions she marched out the front door, suitcase in hand, advising us all sternly that she was "leaving" and would not be back. I remember waiting for hours with my subdued siblings, watching for her return from the front window. When she did come back, she would go straight to bed and not speak to us until the next day. My father would open cans of soup for dinner in the kitchen.

The apartment was dark, all mahogany and blue-green carpets that reminded me of stormy ocean waters at night. My mother occasionally would place thumbtacks in the carpet faceup to stop us from chasing each other from room to room. The neighbors downstairs complained often, and the superintendent, Howard, who liked my parents, would ring our front door bell to let them know of the problem. Howard wore white undershirts with stained armpits, a tool belt with hammers, screwdrivers, and packets of nails weighing down his hips, and perpetually carried a mug of coffee with him.

One of the last times Howard came by, I could see my father's shoulders slump as he leaned against the doorframe and talked to him quietly on the porch. Soon after, my parents started house hunting.

My parents bought their first house when I was ten. It was a three-bedroom bungalow on Seventy-Fifth Street in

Southwest Portland, with a large picture window looking out to the street. The street was in unincorporated Washington County, which meant the county never maintained it. It was mostly gravel, with patches of cement applied over the largest potholes by the retired folks who lived on the street.

I remember doing cartwheels on the front lawn as my parents shook the realtor's hand for the last time, the keys lying flat and burnished on my mother's left palm. The house had been built in 1942, and most of the original interior remained, but the four steps to the two bedrooms over the garage seemed like an afterthought. Outside, there were well-established rhododendrons in the front yard, a Japanese maple to the left of the driveway, and a monstrous arbor vitae hedge more than eight feet tall, separating our property from the neighbors. The kitchen was full of peeling wallpaper in winsome shades of dusty orange and lime green, vinyl flooring in a dizzying geometric pattern, and particle-wood cabinets painted yellow with black wrought iron handles. There was a wide fireplace and mantel in the living room, and all five of us slept there in our sleeping bags the first night, roasting marshmallows. We three children silently observed our parents clinking wineglasses in a toast, their eyes full of tenderness and relief.

The third bedroom was turned into my father's study off the kitchen, and it took three men to wrangle his vintage oak desk into what would become his hideaway, where he usually had a cup of black instant coffee close at hand. You could smell the smoke from his forbidden (by my mother) cigarettes trailing out the door that never fully shut and through which you could hear Art Farmer playing softly on the radio.

My sister and I shared the bedroom overlooking the driveway; my parents had the bedroom next to it, with a view to the eternally soppy backyard. At the base of the stairs to our rooms was an oversize closet, just roomy enough for a narrow bed and bureau. My little brother slept there, cozy as a kitten.

There was never any money in our household, and I don't know where my parents sourced the money for the down payment. As I grew, I learned about making ends meet from observing my mother at the kitchen table poring over her checkbook and an assortment of bills, adding up figures and physically putting cash into various jars labeled "food," "kids' extracurriculars," "fun," "utilities," and so forth. My father would stand behind her and rub her shoulders. "Come on, Sandra. Time for bed," he'd murmur, moving her hair off her neck. Money was a mystery to him. He had left home at sixteen, his parents strict to the point of cruelty, ardent in their belief in God, and repulsed by his creativity and his atheism. He affably followed my mother into a world of children and routines, which she oversaw.

Some events in your childhood scar you in a way that you are not aware of until later in life. It seems humans are drawn to the same well of experience time and time again, choosing unconsciously to revisit what led to the scarring in the first place. We encounter the same repeated event, just with

different players and different scenery. Perhaps we're drawn
to another chance to sort it out, to react differently and ease
the pressure of history. I had thought by my late thirties that
I was finally able to process the event of a remodel without panic over the frightening chaos I associated with it. At
Stratford I would discover I was wrong.

I was an innately neat child. My sister was not. Her version of cleaning our room (required every Sunday after we
rose and before we could go into the rest of the house) was
shoving piles of worn clothing under her twin bed or between
her sheets. Her motivation was low. She didn't care much
about leaving our room or having smooth bedclothes. Her
most frequent posture was curled up in bed with her favorite blanket and her bedraggled pink elephant, Timmy. She
loved sugar, and wrappers of Blow Pops, Lemon Heads, and
Jawbreakers could be found tucked away like lost treasures
between the bed and the wall.

I did my best to smooth the handmade quilt on my own
bed. I would arrange my stuffed-bear collection in a way that
encouraged their sense of community and saved space for me
to sit sideways on the bed and read. I hung my clothes on my
side of our closet and put clean T-shirts in my dresser drawer.
I did struggle with my desk. I was an enthusiastic writer from
a young age, and I had a series of handwritten journals lined
up on my one bookshelf and a collection of books and ruled
notebooks spread below. Words and ideas spilled forth from
my head, finding their way to any empty page that would
accept it. Writing was a never-ending marathon. Any sense

of completion evaded me. This was long before I developed carpal tunnel syndrome in part from gripping my pen so tight and so often, and before I acquired my first word processor during my freshman year of college.

After a few years of living in close quarters in our new home, my parents had somehow managed to save up enough money to break ground on the addition they had envisioned when we first moved in. I craved the tranquility and solitude that I could only find when my siblings were out of the house. The impact of the messy, drawn-out remodel, accomplished in fits and starts as the money became available, was devastating.

At first, friends of my father's did the work at our house on the weekends. Some were teachers I knew from school; some were strangers, but they all had some experience in construction or were just handy. I was shy about having any of them in our home, embarrassed by our used furniture and the mismatched coffee cups they drank from while on break.

First, the foundation was dug in the backyard that was invariably too muddy to even kick a soccer ball. Cement was poured, rebar placed. I observed the work from the side yard, munching on toast or a bowl of cottage cheese. If any of the workers waved at me, I'd jump at being noticed and slink back into the house.

The process of raising a two-story, 1,000-square-foot addition was like building a second house and took more than a year. I was fourteen by then and angsty. My sister had moved up to Seattle to apprentice with the Pacific Northwest Ballet. I gained full control of our bedroom in her absence, locking the door against the rest of the world, smoking clove cigarettes out my window, and listening to John Coltrane late into the night. While the framework of the addition was going up, however, my parents' relationship was splintering. Not privy to the details, I threw myself into my schoolwork and sports, transferring the vast discomfort of my adolescence and the unsettled house into my journals and a newfound habit of eating to excess.

The day came when the wall separating our house from the addition was removed. My father took the first whack at it with a heavy mallet, his blue eyes full of mirth. My brother and I were given crowbars and instructions on how to pull the wall away. Behind us, my mother directed the operation like a flight attendant. The mess was unbearable.

After we broke down the wall, life on Seventy-Fifth Street was never the same. The money for the project must have run low, along with my parents' desire to stay together. Construction continued, however. A thick piece of plastic nailed to an overhead two-by-four functioned as the door into the new section, an attempt to keep heat from leaking from the original house into the uninsulated addition. The master bathroom was completed about three months later. We children could now use the new tub, and I would lounge in it under bubbles for hours, wielding the shower hose on my feet and chest like a personal masseuse.

By the time my sister came home from Seattle, injured and unable to continue dancing, I was seventeen. The sheetrock was finally up in the addition, and my parents had moved in, despite unfinished floors and windows and naked light bulbs hanging from the ceiling. I felt as if I had been inhaling sawdust for half of my life. The unfinished house mirrored the unfinished girl that was me. I was ashamed to have my friends over, though I had known them since kindergarten. I could hardly bear my mother's weeping from the recesses of the addition late at night. Nor the grim set of my father's mouth when I looked for him in his new, vast study upstairs, where his massive desk had somehow been carried up (by giants, I could only assume) and his scattered papers were anchored by a cold coffee mug.

The chaos in the house reflected the burgeoning cracks in the family. All five of us eventually went our separate ways. But the anxiety prompted by the remodel of our family home would resurface during my first marriage and again while I was at Stratford.

8

ARLIE AND ELLEN

Beyond our five-person unit, there were a few other family members who touched my early life and colored the expectations I lived with as an adult. Until I was nine or ten, my uncle Arlie and my auntie Ellen were elders in my family who I revered yet did not know deeply. The woman I sought to be, in my little girl's heart, was some combination of those two souls. Yet I had only a surface understanding of who they were and the lives they had lived. I perceived their talents, their culture, and their grace as something from a bygone era, something I would never attain, given my family and the era that I was born in.

My father had run away from home when he was sixteen. His mother and stepfather were religious zealots, thoroughly convinced that my father and his stepbrother (the same age, born on the same day) were sinners of the highest order. The boys were made to sleep in the barn among the farm animals, and my father would wake to his mother's face bearing down over his, sniffing hard for the smell of booze or smoke, her expression as menacing as a Rottweiler watching a mail carrier from the living room window.

He did not run far. My "uncle" Arlie was my father's high school drama teacher, a gentle and articulate man in his midthirties who had been to war in Germany and stayed on afterward in Vienna to indulge in one of his greatest passions, the opera. Arlie liked cats and young men but did not mistreat any of them, taking strays of both kinds into his home, giving them a bed, food, intellectual conversation, and a quiet space to grow. His home was perched near the banks of the Luckiamute River in Bridgeport, Oregon, where he had lived with his mother, Vintie, since he returned from Europe.

Vintie was barely 55 inches tall, and her thick gray braid reached down her back nearly to her heels. Her upper lip sported a mustache that was hard to not stare at. She always wore a long burgundy skirt and white shirt and the kind of black boots that required a buttonhook to close. She looked as if she had just jumped off a covered wagon that had rattled across the country.

Vintie and Arlie slept in the two bedrooms of the "main house," a ramshackle clapboard home with no insulation, a woodstove, and a sunroom where books covered every wall and filled every corner. My father and a varying group of young men straining toward adulthood had twin beds to choose from in rooms over the garage. Unlike my grandparents' barn, these rooms were heated and had windows, and my father had a key. Trust and kindness must have felt as foreign to him as the German words Arlie occasionally spoke to his cats as they cuddled on his lap.

My father graduated from high school with newfound self-confidence and admission to the honors program at the University of Oregon, but he stayed in touch with Arlie who was directing several plays at Western Oregon University in Monmouth and also corralling his students on the high school stage. My mother was Arlie's director's assistant, the collaborator he had always dreamed of, efficient, maternal, and creative. The two worked together in perfect unison; the budding actors flourished under their tutelage.

My mother had obtained her master's degree in teaching from Western Oregon University, and she was active in theater on campus. She took the lead role in several plays, playing Alma in Tennessee Williams's *Summer and Smoke* and Beatrice in *A View from the Bridge*. My mother relished the theater and the outlandish and moody friends she hung with. She was a mother figure even then, providing solace for many struggling young actors after the curtain went down. She would help them rehearse their lines, and on opening night the electricity that connected them all would be evident on stage. They would act as if their lives depended on it, while the audience sat expectantly in their seats. Afterward they'd gather in stuffy, smoke-filled apartments, wine and gin poured into glasses, their laughter and relief flowing out the open windows.

One night, at one of the after-parties that ran on until the bottles were empty and dawn licked at the doorstep, Arlie introduced my father to my mother. She was twenty-eight, already married and divorced twice. He was twenty-one. My father's blue eyes met my mother's hazel ones. They turned toward each other in conversation, their young figures casting lithe shadows against the wall. Arlie tiptoed to the kitchen for a nightcap before slipping out the door into his pickup truck and home to his cats. My parents married three months later, in front of a justice of the peace.

When I was five or six, my parents took note of my delight in dressing up, my facility for the English language, and my voracious reading. They called Uncle Arlie and set up a date for dinner and the ballet. He arrived around 5 p.m. on a Saturday evening, dapper in his suit and silk, open-collared shirt. It was 1973, and in my memory a feeling of grooviness permeated the era. Clothing, food, and speech were all more laid back than before. People were having fun, moving with a jauntiness and optimism that had just started to replace the angst of the Vietnam era.

For my outing with Arlie, I dressed in my prettiest of dresses, probably velvet red, with a lace collar sewn by my mother. I had shiny patent-leather shoes, a tan faux fur coat, and my white rabbit muff. I was ready.

Uncle Arlie took my hand and let me sit in the front seat of his car. We dined at the Old Spaghetti Factory, where I was careful to watch which fork to use for my salad and how to spoon and twirl my pasta. I was excited by the sights and sounds of people out on the town, spending money, having others wait on them. Uncle Arlie talked to me about books, ballet dancers, and the theater. I felt grown up.

At the ballet Arlie suggested I sit on top of my coat to see better. As the auditorium hushed and the spotlights came up on the maroon curtain, I held my breath. Slowly the curtains parted, revealing a single dancer in repose, wearing a tutu, her legs ending in pointe shoes, and her hair in a tight bun. The orchestra fluttered to life and the music washed over me like warm water. I was straining to stay awake, but I would never let Uncle Arlie see how sleepy I had become with the excitement of it all. I wanted to be invited back, to always be invited back. I was a small, earnest girl, sitting upright and paying attention, not knowing what it was just yet that she loved.

Arlie and I made the ballet an annual event. One year we went to the opera, but I did fall asleep that time, and Arlie took note. Every now and then my father and I would take a Sunday drive out to Bridgeport, to Arlie's home. Vintie was always there, cooking something in the kitchen, no matter our arrival time. She was a kisser. Her mustache softly brushed my nose.

Vintie and Arlie's home was one I wanted to crawl inside and never leave. I was comforted by all the books. The furniture was old and large, begging one to curl up and fall asleep under an afghan. Vintie would serve fresh lemonade, quite sour, in small Russian glasses on a tin, cloth-covered tray. Outside, lawn furniture sprawled across the grass. Under one tree was a simple Victorian chair, meant for reading in quiet, away from the others. Under another hung an old tire swing. Besides my father and me, there were always random guests drifting in and out, and the sound of the Luckiamute River muffled conversation.

Later in the day Vintie would bring out brown bottles of beer, some crackers, and sliced cheese. I'd lay on my back under my favorite tree close to the adults, listening to their talk—Uncle Arlie's thoughtful and erudite voice, perhaps a woman reciting poetry she had recently written, my father's gentle praise. I wrote lines of poetry in my mind, capturing them that night in my journal after my father and I had returned home.

Those nights I would dream about dancers holding books in their hands, old women in white nightgowns floating across the room and bearing trays of drinks, and purring cats swishing around my bare, mosquito-bitten legs.

///////////////

Auntie Ellen was my mother's father's oldest sister. There were eleven children in the Ritter family, which had emigrated to the United States from Germany. Ellen was the oldest and Arno, my grandfather, was the youngest. I knew in between were Cookie, Pearl, and Alma, but none of the others. I don't know if they stayed back in Germany, moved outside of Oregon, or were buried with the rest of the family in Bethany, on the acre of land set aside for the Ritter clan in a private cemetery overseen by a caretaker. I only ever met Ellen and Arno.

Ellen took care of Arno as a boy and off and on into

his late twenties, when he met Grandma Jo. Grandpa Arno's strong farmer's hands were like a vise, and he had a bit of a mean streak. After visiting him and Grandma, we grandchildren would return home with a sore shoulder, where he had pinched us to say hello.

My mom said Grandpa Arno had killed a man in a bar fight in his early twenties and spent some time in jail. After that, though, his life changed. For one thing, he took up square dancing. He wore brightly colored shirts and a bolo tie to the dances, and his handsome chin and stern gaze attracted ladies who tiptoed across the room to meet him. Grandma Jo had his heart from the first time he saw her, with her raven curls, generous bosom, and athletic legs. And Grandpa Arno was Grandma's true love, the man she had waited for until she was practically an old maid at age twenty-seven.

They were well suited as a couple. They danced and danced and played golf and swam. They camped and shot elk, farmed, and sat together on the davenport in the winter and on the swinging couch on the covered patio in the summer, listening to the creak of the rusty springs and the chirping of crickets out in the grass. To me, Grandma was a sweet, busty girl who never left the farm. Her hands were arthritic from sewing, cooking, swaddling three daughters, splitting wood, and hanging wet laundry in the wind.

Grandma Jo's command of the domestic arts was beyond my comprehension, since by the late 1970s, home economics had virtually disappeared from the high school curriculum. My own mother astonished me with the things she knew how to do. Both Grandma and Mom could thread a needle with their eyes closed and turn out a princess costume, ballet tutu, overalls, or knapsack within a few hours. They could transform any vegetable, fruit, or protein into a meal or some canned/dried/frozen form of nourishment into something that would delight all of us at breakfast a month or two later. They knit, crocheted, did needlepoint and cross-stitch, quilted, wove on a loom, and spun yarn on a wheel.

Until I was a teenager, Grandma did all her sewing on a sewing machine with a foot pedal. She also drove her car with two feet: The left foot was for the brake and the clutch, and the right for the gas. Grandma was sturdy and warm, indelicate but gentle. She could handle a gun. She golfed three over par, plowed the fields right next to Grandpa Arno in a matching tractor, and took her turn driving the motor home when they started making winter trips down to the California desert in their sixties.

Her sister-in-law, Auntie Ellen, was something else altogether. She had moved from the family farm in Bethany to Portland, when she was just nineteen. She went to secretarial school at night and worked in a woolen mill during the day. Once she got her legal secretary's certificate, she took a job with a city judge and never looked back. My father insists Ellen was the first woman in Portland to obtain her driver's license. She drove her Oldsmobile with white gloves, the windows open, and often with one of her sisters by her side. Once out of town she would step on the gas pedal and let it fly, her hair barely contained under a scarf.

Ellen was always stylish, and in her younger days she wore her hair short and dressed as a flapper in the evenings, wearing silk pumps and a beaded sleeveless dress with a dropped waist. She was just five feet tall, had a boyish figure and flawless snow-white skin. Her hand, when she held yours, was both tender and firm. She had many admirers and was never without a date on Saturday night.

In fact, Ellen went on to marry four times. I heard talk of an alcoholic, an abuser, and a shiftless ne'er-do-well. Then there was Daddy Mac, Ellen's last husband. I have a photo of the two of them standing in front of their yellow house in Portland. Mac was a dapper older man in a gray suit, wearing a hat like a detective in a James Cain novel, his arm loose around Ellen's waist, trying to close the foot of space between them. Mac died by his own gun.

Like Grandma and Grandpa, Ellen loved to dance. She could play the piano and the accordion. She was a charming hostess, and everything about her was fashionable and clean. Her 1940s bungalow was decorated in her favorite colors of lemon yellow and lime green. She had a formal dining room and well-cared-for furniture, unlike my house, which was filled with a mix of furniture handed down or picked up at a garage sale.

Ellen's pink lipstick from Avon was always the same. Her bottle of Arpege by Lanvin never seemed to empty, and she always smelled like violets and lilies. Later a curly white wig covered her thinning hair in public.

Sometimes I was lucky enough to spend the night with

her, and she was not shy as I watched her get comfortable after dinner. She would remove her large bra, her polyester pants, and her knee-high nylon stockings. She would button up her housecoat and, at last, pull the pins attaching the wig to her own hair. Her eyes were dry and sensitive to the light, she explained to me as she put drops from a little bottle into them. After brushing her thin white hair back off her face, she would don a green visor, and we would settle ourselves on the couch next to the crystal candy dish with lemon drops and mints to watch Lawrence Welk.

When my family came for dinner, Ellen cooked the same meal every time: baked ham, green beans and butter, hot rolls, and mashed potatoes. For most of my childhood that was my favorite meal. I dreamed about it both before and after we went to her house. After dinner she would play the accordion, while my parents sipped sherry and Caitlin, Josh, and I lay on the soft carpet in front of the TV. Sometimes we would get to watch *Donny & Marie* or *The Carol Burnett Show* before our parents herded us to the car, apologizing to Auntie Ellen for the lateness of the evening. I would hug her as though I never wanted to leave her. Her warm hands would cup my face in goodbye.

Auntie Ellen and I shared almost the same birthday. They were actually three days (and at least sixty years) apart, but we were both born in April under the same sign (Taurus), and in her mind and mine we had a special bond.

Every year on my birthday she would phone me and arrange for our overnight together and a birthday outing.

My middle-child tendency to think I could never be the center of attention would melt like an ice cube on a bonfire. I am pretty sure I would clap my hands with delight. In part it was knowing what to expect. I was always soothed if I knew the routine in advance, and I also knew the day would include all the things I found wonderful.

My father would drop me off at her house at 10 a.m. on a Saturday. We would take the bus, because by then Aunt Ellen was not driving anymore; her cataracts caused the world to appear dusted in fog, and she had given her Oldsmobile to my parents.

My graceful, well-mannered, sophisticated aunt would be wearing white gloves and carrying a vinyl purse with two gold clasps over her wrist. Her pearl necklace matched her pearl earrings. Together we would ride the bus to Lloyd Center, the shopping mall a few miles from her house with the ice-skating rink in the center and a ceiling open to the sky.

Or we would take the bus downtown to Meier & Frank, with its nine floors of apparel, cookware, furniture, and jewelry. On those days Auntie Ellen bought each of us a new dress and shoes. For me it was usually something with flowers and ruffles along with patent-leather Mary Janes. For herself she preferred a lime-green or sunny-yellow dress with cap sleeves, a full skirt, and a cinched waist. Shoes were comfortable matching flats with no more than a two-inch heel.

Then, as I proudly carried my own Meier & Frank shopping bag, the dress wrapped in white tissue paper and my shoes tucked away in their cardboard box with a lid, we'd ascend to the tenth floor and the Georgian Room. Auntie Ellen would walk up to the hostess's podium and quietly ask for a table for two. I did not have to be told twice to put the white cloth napkin on my lap. She ordered a sherry and I asked for a Shirley Temple, and it was placed in front of me like the most delicious Manhattan I would order in my future.

Later that night I would lie in bed in her front room, where guests always slept, watching the headlights from cars wash across the window. Ellen's Underwood typewriter was to the right of my head. I could turn and see its dark outline on the writing desk where she typed letters to family and friends at seventy-five words per minute.

Ellen did not have any children of her own. When she tucked me in, she touched my face and patted the sheet by my side. I still remember how I loved her.

9

EUROPE, THE FIRST TIME

When I was thirteen, I peed in my sleeping bag in a tent on a concrete slab in a German campground. That night turned out to be another pivotal moment in my young life.

My parents were not world travelers, but they appreciated the fine arts, the theater, the ballet, galleries, and fine food from Europe. They tried to pass that on to us kids. So when my mother read an article in *The Oregonian* about two teachers in a Portland suburb who led a dozen or so middle schoolers on a summer trip to Europe, she signed me up. It would be a month-long trip. On a bicycle.

I worked for weeks babysitting to earn the thousand-dollar ticket to "ride," so to speak. I borrowed one of my neighbor's bikes, a real road bike with a narrow seat that I came to dislike within the first week, approaching it each morning like a wild horse I had to mount without a saddle. And my mother spent the better part of a month sewing paniers and a front pack to haul the meager list of belongings we were authorized to bring.

My best friend, Hallie, signed up, too, because I asked her to go, and she was always up for an adventure. Her mother smiled at me and wrote a check for me to take to the school-teachers along with my own. I loved Hallie for never making me feel inferior about lack of money. She used to join me on occasion when I babysat, and while I looked on it quite seriously as a job that I could not afford to make mistakes at, she would fly into the children's playroom and immediately get down on the floor to play with the kids. She was just as serious as I was in so many other ways, but she had a flair for meeting children at their level that I lacked. My instinct was to mother them intensely, with generous but stern love, healthy amounts of food and exercise, and activities that stimulated their growing brains.

That night in Germany, Hallie and I worked hard to raise our shared tent on concrete. Who had ever heard of such a thing? We were used to camping in the Oregon woods, clearing the uneven forest floor to hammer tent pegs into. Not once had we encountered concrete. Now we were exhausted after a day of biking and were mildly annoyed with each other. That wasn't too surprising. Spending too many days being slightly uncomfortable in a foreign country often affects friendships.

After dark Hallie and I made our way to the women's bathroom, past tents packed closely together, listening to the chortling and guffawing from various picnic tables where folks had gathered for one last beer. The bathroom, which lacked doors on the toilet stalls, was completely jammed with

European women brushing their teeth, helping each other with their hair, and squatting to pee. A glance was all we needed. Hallie and I turned around and ran back to our tent.

Later that night I had a dream where I was being chased by something—I don't know what—down a narrow street somewhere in Europe. Old women shouted at me over flower boxes from their windows, but I could not understand what they were saying as they spoke some foreign tongue I did not recognize. I was terrified. And I had to urinate. I had to urinate so badly my bladder threatened to burst. When I yelled out loud, Hallie elbowed me hard in the ribs, and I woke up. The inside of my sleeping bag was peculiarly wet and cold.

"Oh, Christ," I swore, punching Hallie back on the arm. We were still swearing freely every chance we had.

"What?" she whispered. Hallie had many talents, and one of them was whispering just loud enough that I could hear her but no one would be disturbed.

"I fucking peed myself!"

Hallie reached out and put her hand over my mouth to shush me. There were tents all around us. We could hear snores.

"What the fuck!" she whispered and then started giggling uncontrollably, tears rolling down her face with the effort to keep her laughing silent. I dropped several more muted f-bombs and then tried to get up, an awkward proposition when you are sitting in a pee-soaked sleeping bag and you can't stand because you're in a pup tent. Meanwhile I was trying to figure out what in the world I was going to do before dawn came and the rest of the people in our group detected my disgrace.

"You can never ever EVER tell anyone!" I whispered ferociously at Hallie as she stuffed her face into her makeshift sweatshirt-pillow. Somehow, I managed to worm my way out of the tent, dragging the offensive nylon sleeping bag with me through the flapped doorway. Like a soldier carrying a wounded member of her platoon, I marched toward the women's restroom. At 3 a.m. the place was all mine, and I turned on the blinding neon lights. Inevitably one malfunctioned, flashing like a police car over the farthest sink.

Hallie had loyally followed me, and she helped me turn my sleeping bag inside out and scrub it with soap. After a while we were overcome with fatigue and, feeling silly, skulked back to our tent like servants finished with their earliest morning chores. I decided to hang the inside-out bag over the top of our tent in hopes it might dry before we got up for breakfast a few hours later. The teachers had us on a strict schedule in order to fulfill the many tourist activities that they had carefully mapped out along our journey. There would be no slacking over a damp sleeping bag in the morning. I pulled on all the clothes I had and shivered on my thin roll-up mat until daylight.

Overnight it drizzled, spraying a mist of rain like someone lightly hosing a small child in a driveway on a hot summer day. Now my entire sleeping bag was soaked through, but at least the rain had removed a layer of suspicion about why the bag was wet. After breakfast I stuffed it into its sack, tied it to the back of my bike with the rest of my belongings, and pedaled into the wind.

That night—indeed, that entire trip abroad—was an indication of how I would meet difficult challenges from then on. Masochistically I would convince myself that anything could be overcome if I only worked at it with the persistence of a prisoner escaping from prison by chiseling at the wall with their fingernails. Traveling in Germany and Denmark those weeks posed a physical challenge I had never faced up until that point. I had saddle sores from the biking, burning pain in my quads and calves, and sunburn on my arms and face.

There were other challenges as well. Except for Hallie, the students on the trip were strangers to me, as were the two teachers. The bubble of the private school I had attended since kindergarten, where my father taught, burst, and I was compelled to interact with people who cared about different things than I did. Being the middle child, I came equipped with certain skills of diplomacy, and I quickly learned how to mask any discomfort over those differences with a measured cheerfulness and acceptance that even I came to believe was real.

That summer produced the first incarnation of my young adult self: an Erin of "after" quite unlike the Erin of "before." Both my mind and body responded to the daily experiences like crops to fertilizer. Certain events were imprinted in my memory bank like pressed flowers in a book: lunch with the queen mother of Denmark at her country home overlooking a valley, at a long table set outside with tulips in wine bottle vases. The bands playing at Tivoli Gardens, where the Danes danced, their eyes closed, their faces turned up to the hot sun. Dozens of churches with cool, silent interiors, like the inside of an old refrigerator on my Grandpa Arno's farm, where he kept his dark brown bottles of Henry Weinhard's beer. Those churches intrigued me, a thirteen-year-old agnostic just beginning to be fascinated by white magic, astrology, and the netherworld. Then there were the pubs where we were allowed small glasses of beer, warm loaves of bread, and hunks of cheese.

After the European trip, I came home with tan muscular legs, a stronger will, and a "c'est la vie" attitude propelling me toward endeavors that I might have shied away from before. My natural tendency had always been to stay in small, safe circles. Now I wanted to swim out into the waves. I was determined. I was suddenly worldly! Brazen! I could take on anything!

10

GRIEVANCES

I could have used some of that adolescent verve in my early days at Stratford. Just showing up at work was proving to be a daily exercise in the unexpected and the unknown. In the more recent past, I had been reliant on stability, on knowing what to expect from my day: coffee in the morning, weekly meetings about forecasts, employee performance, and new software implementation; afternoons catching up on emails and marking up underwriting reports from staff. At Stratford, however, the more I tried to exert control over my day, the less control I actually had. There were days I wasn't sure I'd be able to get to the bathroom or make it to meetings on time, let alone eat lunch.

I resorted to feeble attempts to block my calendar and close my office door, spreading a cloth napkin over my lap and brewing a cup of tea from a metallic red insta-heat kettle I acquired at Target. After my kettle became known to some of the other staff members, it almost immediately transformed into a community item. I would come into my office and discover someone fixing themselves a cup. Nothing at

Stratford was sacred or personal for long. All property eventually belonged to everyone.

When I was forced to stay late in the evenings, I would light a juniper-scented candle by the window and nibble on organic dark chocolate and sip coffee from the kitchen, handed to me with a bright smile from the night cook.

Periodically I would ask one of the housekeepers, Pam, to clean my office while I was out to a meeting. When I came back, the scent of Lemon Pledge met my nostrils like a soothing balm, and I could see the tracks of the vacuum cleaner in the carpet and enjoy the clear Windex-sprayed glass of my window, through which I could see residents ambling by on the sidewalk outside. For all the attempts the residents made to gain my attention, not once did anyone knock on that window. It was as if once they were outside the building, life inside Stratford was gone from their consciousness. The outdoor world was so vast and beguiling as to command every bit of their attention. I could just have been a woman in a painting looking out from the frame.

Late-night sessions in my office came close to peaceful. Dinner was served from 4:30 to 6 p.m., and many residents returned to their apartments soon after. The med nurses made their evening rounds; caregivers helped residents off with their shoes and clothes and into their pajamas. Avid readers might settle into easy chairs with an afghan tucked across their lap. In the hall you might hear old reruns of *Family Feud* through the door of a resident's room. A small group of two or three residents would amble out to the designated smoking area, the glowing ends of their cigarettes beacons of orange light in the darkness.

The stack of grievances in my inbox constantly demanded my attention, though. They came in various forms: loosely folded handwritten notes, letters sealed in envelopes, emails of any length, sometimes several from the same person sent within minutes of each other. I had notes of phone calls and in-person meetings in my office or in the large conference room. These meetings might include a resident, their friends or family members, and sometimes the ombudsmen, a retired married couple who took their duties quite seriously. I've always been a copious notetaker, fearing that I won't remember a thing unless it's written down, so I had stacks of notes to go with each grievance. It was my task to respond to each of them within a prescribed time frame and with a sound action or recompense. Otherwise my employer or I would be subject to regulatory action.

It was never entirely clear what might happen if I failed to address a grievance properly or who, in fact (other than the resident with the complaint), could analyze my response for its overall appropriateness. Grievances were a nebulous matter, fraught with subjectivity, and to me they represented one of the most bewildering aspects of managing the facility.

I could never really know if I had satisfied the resident who filed a grievance. Actually, I am certain in most cases I did not; my sense was that a good portion of the residents lived in a perpetual state of dissatisfaction. The repetitive nature of some of the grievances only made things worse.

Several residents seemed to enjoy the very process of filing a grievance, as if it were a sport. It was as if I were on a Ferris wheel of grievances. I would respond to a resident's complaints, and two days later they would be back with more. One resident, Mary Catherine, would drop a note at the receptionist's desk daily for me.

"Milton Baxter stared at me crossly over breakfast," wrote Mary Catherine. "I think he's a mean old coot."

The next day she wrote, "Eldonna Gervais stole Myrtle Shannon's favorite earrings. The aquamarine ones, I think. Maybe it was her yellow topaz ones. Anyway, ask Myrtle."

The day after that she wrote, "I am very lonely and sad. No one likes me here. I wish we could have sherbet every day on the menu."

And later that day, she added, "I asked for sherbet because the doc says I am not supposed to have dairy. Tell Albert [the head cook] he should stop giving me ice cream. Also, I really like the caregiver Irina. Can I have her on my floor all the time?"

I also got complaints from a long-standing resident named Leo, who was in moderately good physical condition but had diminishing mental health. Leo rarely spoke to anyone, and when he did, he'd mutter in a garbled and angry fashion that was difficult to decipher. With a newspaper or magazine tucked under an arm, he strode the halls of Stratford in his worn camel-colored cardigan sweater and loose-fitting tan pants held up by an oversize belt. His bushy gray brows were permanently furrowed. Periodically he would drop an epistle at my office door; if Jewell or Jeannine were away, he would boldly peek in to see if I was seated inside.

Several times I was at my computer, and upon seeing him I would invite him in to chat, but Leo would wave me away as if I were a swarm of bees, a startled look softening his face. It was rumored he had once been a history teacher or a newspaper columnist. Several residents claimed he was a die-hard Communist and had tried to convert them to Marxism. His grievances did have a manifesto quality to them. He wrote many pages criticizing the way Stratford was run and how it attracted a contingent of society that he firmly believed did not belong there.

For the most part, Leo wanted justice and peace. The latter I could certainly understand, but his diatribes about justice were less clear, making it difficult for me to sort out what was a grievance and what was simply a political statement. He used all capital letters and added exclamation points at the end of nearly every sentence, which left me feeling as if I had undergone a tirade, even though I rather enjoyed reading his messages, full as they were with deep thoughts.

"I MUST DECLARE THIS ENTIRE BUILDING A COMPLETE DISGRACE!" he stated. "MILTON BAXTER MAKES IT IMPOSSIBLE TO DIGEST ONE'S MEAL WITH HIS SCOWLING NATURE! THERE IS NOT A QUIET SPOT TO READ A PAPER! THERE IS TOO MUCH GARBAGE AND EQUIPMENT BLANKETING THE HALLS! I CAN HARDLY NAVIGATE A PATH FROM ONE END OF THE BUILDING TO THE OTHER! ALSO, MY ROOM IS COLD!

JUSTICE SHOULD BE SERVED TO THE WHOLE LOT OF THEM BECAUSE IF THEY ARE OPPRESSED THEN THEY SHOULD RISE UP AND DO SOMETHING ABOUT IT SO THAT EVERYONE GETS A WARM BOWL OF SOUP!"

I empathized with Leo's grievances, as well as Mary Catherine's. I, too, would have found Stratford an exceedingly difficult place to live.

There was a general format I was required to follow in responding to grievances. Address the individual. Apologize for their discomfort or however they experienced the problem. Describe the grievance as you understood it. Provide a solution.

If the matter was serious—say, if something was allegedly stolen or someone was physically threatened or harmed—other measures were required, such as filing a police report and an incident report with the state. For more routine matters, such as (a) "so-and-so ate from my bowl of soup at lunch," or (b) "I asked for my mail and Jewell refused to get it for me because she was on the phone," I would whip out a letter with the appropriate solution:

A. I will ask so-and-so to please only eat the food served to them. You also have the option of eating at another table.

B. Jewell has several tasks to complete throughout the day. One of these is answering the phone. If you could wait next time until she completes her call, I am sure she would be happy to get your mail for you.

With more complex or unusual complaints, I went to great lengths to analyze the issue at hand and consider how I might address it. Often, I would interview other residents to get a better picture of what happened (there were always witnesses), and I would discuss my impressions with caregivers, our social worker, nurses, and the doctor. The ombudsmen were frequently in the facility, looking for opportunities to chat with me about their "observations." Sometimes it seemed they spent more time stirring the pot than providing support to a resident with a grievance. The activity director was able to provide objective insights, since she spent much of her day interacting with various residents on outings to Walmart, over bingo, and in watercolor class, among other scheduled events.

In the end attending to grievances was a draining and disappointing process. Rarely, if ever, did I believe a resident was happy with the solution provided. Instead I sensed that the power they felt in filing the grievance was really the most important factor of all. It was the power to let someone know you were hurt, afraid, uncomfortable, and mad. Once they let me know that, they could move on with their day.

11

BALANCING ACTS

I was perched on the thin roller-paper-covered exam table with its empty stirrups facing me, my feet dangling over the side. I was waiting for Dr. Wang to return to the room as a wall clock ticked softly behind me. I already knew what the ultrasound would indicate: not a plump sphere with a heartbeat but a flattened version of itself, something wrong in the nucleus that should have been a merger of Jay and me.

It was late November, and I had been working at Stratford for close to a month. I figured I had gotten pregnant in late August. My memory of my last period was blurry, and I hadn't been keeping track. But deep down I knew something was wrong. My body didn't seem to be laying the foundations I recalled from my prior pregnancies. I hadn't gained any weight, wasn't slowing down. I had been here before, during my first marriage, with the pregnancy between Camille and Gunnar that ended in miscarriage. I also felt strangely removed from the idea of the new baby. By this time in the first trimester, I had had silent conversations with both Camille and Gunnar. They were already a part of me, a part of our family, and I was cheering them on as they took over my womb.

Dr. Wang was petite and efficient, her thick black hair pulled back in a ponytail, her speech sharp and composed. (I had chosen her because her profile on the OB-GYN website said she was married to one of my favorite local jazz musicians, who played the saxophone with gusto and closed-eye passion.) She gave me the news straight and finished with a warm smile. She was not lacking in compassion, but I knew she had delivered similar news more times than she could remember.

And I already had sensed Jay's and my baby wasn't there. Its existence was like a flash of light from the hall, when someone opens the bedroom door in the middle of the night, and then it's gone and you go back to sleep. Your memory of it is just a dream.

I was forty-two. The door had closed; we would not be here again. I had yearned for our child together, but that yearning had also been mingled with fear. Fear we were too old and tired, fear the baby would have something wrong, fear that another being would pierce the carefully constructed, merged family we had worked so hard to achieve, that last Jenga piece added to the stack that caused everything to come crashing down. I knew in my bones it had been a mistake to go forward with hopes for another child, but I loved Jay even more for his willingness to try. Over the four years we had been together, I had discovered his way of loving me was based on a desire to know me deeply and to help me remove the obstacles I self-imposed on the life I wanted.

Jay was always capable of seeing through the morass of weeds that kept me, or anyone he loved, from getting what they wanted. If Gunnar mentioned he had fun rock climbing with a friend, Jay would take him to get his own harness and climbing shoes and research the rock-climbing walls in town. If Ava said she thought about becoming a filmmaker, he'd sign her up for a two-week intensive summer program at the Portland Art Museum. Sometimes we would delight in his efforts to help us; other times we would balk, feeling unready.

Jay was never afraid, though there were consequences for him. Sometimes what the other person wanted, the thing he helped guide them to, was not what he himself wanted. I was still learning that he would not speak up if my needs ran contrary to his own. He always put me first.

When I told him that night that the baby was not growing, and we could wait or go ahead to schedule a dilation and curettage, I watched as tears came to his eyes. I know they were for me and for us. I can only imagine everything else going through his mind.

"We should do what you want to do, sweetheart," he said, holding me close as we sat in our kitchen.

"I don't know," I said, shaking my head slowly. "I can't even think right now. Everything is so insane at Stratford. I just can't get my arms around it all." It had started to dawn on me then that I probably would not have survived a pregnancy working at Stratford.

"You don't have to decide now. Give it a week or so," Jay said. That night I lay in bed watching the bright light of the full moon float through our thin blinds and across the ceiling as Jay held my hand in his sleep.

After the miscarriage, something seemed to shift. Jay and I had moved in together abruptly and with little contemplation, and we had not looked back. It had never even occurred to me that our life together might be temporary. In fact, Jay had proposed to me over the prior summer, just before he lost his job, at the restaurant where we had our first date in June 2006. We always intended to marry but had not rushed to plan anything, certainly not in those first months of losing our jobs. Then we were distracted by my getting pregnant and finding new jobs and merging households, and somehow more than a year had passed. When I had a rare quiet moment for reflection one day, driving home from Stratford, I decided it was best we get married, and soon. I can't explain the sense of urgency that suddenly possessed me, but when I told Jay, he did not disagree.

"It's best for the children," he said. This made perfect sense to me. For an agnostic like me, marriage is less about religion and all the promises and bonds it entails, and more about pragmatism and the assurance that formally partnering with someone you love is better than being alone.

Jay and I were Generation Xers, born at the end of the baby boom generation, when people who had babies generally got married first, as if a marriage certificate ensured that each of you would be staying around to raise the child.

Getting married was a message we wanted to send to the rest of the world, including the children we already had: "You can count on the two of us always being together now. What you might need from one of us you can equally get from the other. We will always take care of you, feed you, guide you, provide you shelter. We will present a united front for you so you can trust that the world is a safe place."

The love Jay and I shared was an unbreakable bond. We rarely quarreled, and most days we would laugh together. When it came to politics, ambition, spirituality, health, and dreams for us and for our children, we generally looked at the world in the same way. Those parts of us that were different we respected in the other and nurtured quietly.

We told the kids that evening we were going to get the wedding plans going. Camille, our thirteen-year-old future event planner and budding artist, went gleefully to work hand-making our invitations, helping devise the guest list, and suggesting everyone's attire. The rushed nature of it all—the wedding was set for seven weeks away—aligned with the pandemonium that existed in every aspect of my life at that time. It almost felt as if one of us were soon shipping off to active combat.

Shortly after Christmas we were dashing about wildly trying to make it all happen. Looking back, I believe I was slightly deranged. Perhaps I viewed the wedding as a watershed for all six of us. An event that would propel us out of the state of bedlam where we were learning to exist by new standards and into a more serene place, like vacationers shooting out of a tunneled water slide into a quiet pool.

I had loved weddings since I was eight and dressed up with my sister, in matching frocks sewn by my mother, for a family friend's wedding. My sister had her Dorothy Hamill wedge hairdo, while my long golden hair was pinned in an updo with two loose strands curled along my cheeks. We held small bouquets of peonies and stood next to the bride and groom for a black-and-white photo.

My adoration of weddings stems from my general love of pomp, fine things, jewels, and all things related to flowers. As a young girl I would play "dress-up" with my friends; we pulled all kinds of delightful items from a trunk in my house and paraded around wearing costume jewelry, three-inch heels, flowing velvet skirts and lacy hats, faux fur wraps, and old wire corsets, as we talked to each other in our best highfalutin voices.

After college, when I finally had a little money to spend on finery for myself, I would shop for a cocktail dress and matching shoes for a holiday party or special event. I basked in the process of getting ready—showering, dabbing scent behind my ears, carefully applying my makeup, and curling my hair. The most cherished aspect of my apparel was my lingerie. I loved getting lacy items tucked between ivory tissues in a box with a satin ribbon. Over time the price and quality of my undergarments increased along with the size of my paychecks. It was one of my private ways of bringing beauty into each day.

Jay and I married on January 16, 2010, in the library of the University Club in Portland. The building dated to just after the turn of the century, and the stone-and-brick 1920s facade reminding me of Manderley, the mansion in Daphne du Maurier's novel *Rebecca*.

I carried dark red roses and wore a gold strapless dress, with my hair down in soft waves. Jay's eyes teared up after I read the vows I had written, as our four children stood alongside us. Our guests filled the narrow room whose walls were covered in books.

I loved the idea of marrying in a library. I've always believed books have protective powers. I could spend hours flipping through volumes or rest my head on a table surrounded by books and feel as if I were among my closest friends. The silence of libraries was full of promise and wonderment.

My only disappointment with the wedding was that Jay wanted no dancing. We did have music to accompany a slide-show of both of us from our childhood to the present day, and I had enjoyed picking out the songs that accompanied the photos that scrolled on a large screen against the wall.

After the ceremony, we had cocktails and passed hors d'oeuvres, then moved into the cornflower-blue dining room where centerpieces of dusty pink roses graced the round tables. People stood up to make toasts. The most charming were those by our two awkward eleven-year-old boys. Cole went first, at ease with his height and the public speaking. Gunnar jumped around like a squirrel and for once was at a loss for words.

Outdoors, the sky went from a windy navy blue to charcoal, as torrents of rain rushed against the old windowpanes.

Our guests started to migrate toward the stairs, and Jay and I held hands and dashed to the Hotel Modera, just across the street. I wore the vintage white mink I had purchased at an antique shop years before; it had a satin lining stitched with the name "Marge."

The next morning, I woke up to Jay holding the left side of his face; his jaw was swollen and red. When he managed to see a dentist two days later, it turned out he had a cracked tooth that took several appointments to repair.

It was one of the first times I observed Jay's stoicism. He endured that aching tooth throughout our wedding and never ever said a word. He was certainly not going to let his bride know about it on her magical day.

12

WHERE'S THE BOSS?

Wendy and I had monthly one-on-one meetings at the ElderHome headquarters in her cool, shadowed office with a narrow window looking out on a damp parking lot and a cluster of trees. The wet dog smell of the building was masked by a strong floral candle burning in the corner. Wendy herself always smelled like a spring shower or a fresh-cut apple.

I did my best during these meetings to put on a confident face and to match her enthusiasm and kindness. Wendy possessed a panache I have never come across, before or since. Her skin was smooth, not a wrinkle anywhere, belying her age, which was the same as mine. She arranged her short chestnut hair in funky gelled spikes that somehow came off as extraordinarily feminine. Her lips were always fuchsia pink. Her clothing was a wild concoction of mixed colors and fabrics like wool, leather, and beads.

There was something about Wendy that made you want to embrace her, or at a minimum follow her like a puppy. She was the sole reason I was able to endure my eighteen months at Stratford. She understood everything. She saw it all, and she acknowledged it before I could even voice my concerns.

"Oh, it's a hot mess over there, Erin, an absolute train wreck," she said after I had plunked myself down in the chair by her desk. Her words flew into the air like sparks from a campfire. It was early December, and the facilities were deep into preparation for the holidays. Stratford had barely finished with construction, and the medical clinic was still without a doctor or head nurse and had yet to open.

"I know this has been hard on you," Wendy added, her cerulean eyes looking straight into my gray-blue ones. The color of my eyes and my hair had prompted one of the residents, Karen, who I had met the day I interviewed at Stratford, to dub me the "ice queen" as I passed her in the hall the previous week.

"I was tryin' to think what you look like to me," said Karen, whose accent curls were a dark, barely discernable purple now, as she periodically changed up the color.

"With that white hair and those piercing blue eyes . . . you the ICE QUEEN!" she blurted out, briefly rousing one of the other residents, Davis Jones. His preferred dozing spot was a chair in the entry, next to a side table with a reading lamp. He peered sternly through sleepy eyes at Karen, then allowed his chin to drift back toward his chest. I looked at Karen quizzically, wondering if she meant it as an insult and decided she was more like a mean girl in the schoolyard putting the new girl through the ropes. She would probably forget the nickname by the next day, though, as it turned out, it would return to her from time to time whenever she noticed my blond hair. The next few times she called me "ice queen," I detected a certain mirth in her tone, a warmth even, suggesting she thought I couldn't help the way I looked or carried myself, and maybe even liked me a little.

"I am here to support you," Wendy was saying. "And so is Sammy. [The ElderHome housing director.] I've asked her to spend more time at Stratford for the next month or so to help you with some of the challenges that continue."

I looked at Wendy, my mind swirling with those challenges. Hiring a head nurse in the clinic, for example. I had interviewed seven people. None were suitable. Either they lacked the experience, or something was just off about them. I had never run across such a bizarre collection of individuals with odd mannerisms, inappropriate and unguarded answers to my interview questions, and poor references or red flags in their backgrounds. For the doctor's position side, we had no applicants at all. A search was now being conducted outside of Oregon.

It dawned on me that it was hardly shocking I had gotten the job at Stratford. Who hires an ops manager—essentially an assisted living facility administrator—with no experience? Desperate people. The collective eagerness on the faces of the group who interviewed me flashed back in my mind. They were like six-year-olds waiting for a chance to whack the piñata at a birthday party.

Staffing generally was a complete disaster. Every day of every week, cooks, caretakers, and house cleaners called in sick or arrived late. At work they hid in closets, smoked with residents, filed worker's compensation claims, gave someone the wrong meds, and angrily quit (often in full view of residents who would hoot and applaud). There was no leverage to keep the staff on the straight and narrow. Plus, they had plenty of difficulties of their own: They were ridiculously underpaid for the work they did. They were often put in harm's way. They had mouths to feed at home and unreliable day care, abusive partners, and beat-up cars in need of costly repairs. They were yelled at routinely by those they were paid to care for, spat on, and subjected to undesired fondling and profanity. A few of them regularly worked double shifts, sixteen-hour days, to make ends meet. They were mostly under the age of thirty, but their bodies and minds were on a par with someone much older, given the stress they underwent from what was asked of them every day.

The greatest challenge at Stratford were the residents themselves, a few of whom actively occupied my time twenty-four hours a day. I would receive phone calls in the dead of night: Jeremy had pulled a knife on Joseph, Dinah had been found unconscious on the floor of her room, Maeve had tried to assault the housekeeper when she tried to clean her room, and so on. Maeve was a hoarder, and the housekeeper, Pam, had made countless attempts to enter her room but generally encountered a blockade. Pam preferred to work the swing shift (2–10 p.m.), and she observed Maeve's comings and goings for several weeks. One night, when she knew Maeve had gone to dinner, Pam grabbed her bucket and supplies and hustled over to Maeve's door. She winked at me in passing, muttering that she was "going in!" Unbeknownst to her, however, Maeve had curried favor with her neighbor Harriet by sharing sweets saved from lunch. Harriet heard Pam's key in Maeve's door followed by the sounds of a vacuum cleaner. She texted Maeve downstairs, and Maeve hustled back up the elevator in a fury. She had somehow managed to acquire a golf club and swung it handily at Pam's head as she entered her room. Pam narrowly escaped, dragging out as much rotting food, "borrowed" clothing, and stacks of newspapers as she could.

A second group of residents, not as rowdy as the first, would come at me in fits and starts. For a week or two they'd keep to themselves, and then suddenly one would snap, and it was all hands on deck to help them. These hidden threats kept me up at night.

The third group encompassed the quiet ones, the introverts, the sweet ones; this group gave me hope and inspired me to hang on, just one more day. I kept thinking it had to get better. It just had to.

As time went on, though, I began to question what exactly I was waiting for. What development, what end goal did I seek? I was a project-oriented person; what I began, I wanted to finish. But what that meant at Stratford eluded me. The person I had always known myself to be was starting to change in not especially comforting ways. I felt raw, as if I were daily being beaten down. Something would come to partially salve me, and then the punishment would start all over again.

I attempted to maintain some normalcy in my home routines. Weekends were still occupied by our kids playing soccer and basketball, grocery shopping, and dinners out with friends. Jay and I went to spin classes at our athletic club if we could get there by 5:30 p.m. during the week, and 10 a.m. on Sundays. I slogged away, nevertheless feeling my rear end increasing in diameter.

Camille had encouraged us to join the Sunset Athletic Club (SAC) over the summer so we could use their outdoor pool, new yoga studio, and fitness areas. I started up yoga again, which I hadn't done since the maelstrom of my divorce seven years earlier. I started Pilates, too. It strengthened my outer core even as my inner core, my spirit, flagged miserably. I looked inward for my strength because I didn't want to burden my strongest supporters: Jay, Camille (my fellow Taurean who shared my persistence), my mother, my lifelong girlfriends, and my old Textron colleagues, who reminded me of what work used to be like and sent emails with coping strategies.

I had been a boss most of my life, whether as team captain, magazine editor, soccer coach, manager, matriarch, or event planner, and I had felt empowered by those positions. At Stratford, despite my title, despite how "big!" a job I had (as Wendy often reminded me), I felt like an imposter. Any natural power I brought to the position was being drained out of me like the battery would of a first-generation flip phone left unplugged overnight. Yet, every morning, the alarm went off, and with concrete will I would move my two feet out from underneath our down comforter and onto the floor. Stratford was calling, and it was time for another day.

13

ETCH A SKETCH

Part of my job as an operations manager for Stratford included running to various meetings held at the other assisted living facilities (ALFs) under the ElderHome umbrella. These other ALFs included buildings of assorted shapes, sizes, and vintages located all over Portland and its outer reaches. Headquarters was in Southeast Portland, in a brick building with uneven floors and a perennially sour smell of wet carpet. Conference rooms were available in each of the buildings, but the spaces were initially hard for me to find; for the first few months I was frequently late to meetings because I had poorly estimated the time it would take me to drive there, and a series of doors would take me from one end of the facility to the other—leading to a left here, a right there, through an atrium or the dining hall, up some stairs and past the nurses' station. Some of the doors would be locked, requiring me to double back to find a caretaker or nurse with a key or pass code to let me through. Keeping track of the countless meetings and where they were held, let alone the topics covered at the meetings, was enough to make me lose my mind.

It reminded me of when I was a child, and Josh, Caitlin, and I each got an Etch A Sketch for Christmas, as did several of my friends at school. For a budding artist, the toy offered an opportunity to show off one's agility at drawing masterpieces. Using two twirling white buttons, you could create lines on a light gray rectangle rimmed in red plastic. You could go back over what you had previously drawn, but you couldn't erase anything without erasing the entire picture. You did so by shaking the tablet violently until the screen cleared. Over time too much clearing of the screen prevented it from being totally cleared, and remnants of your prior efforts would stick to the corners and random spots in the middle.

Sometimes the work of a skilled Etch A Sketcher was astonishing. Friends created castles with flags and moats, dragons breathing fire, a still life of fruit and vegetables in a bowl, and more. I myself would start out mindfully enough, attempting to draw a simple house, trees, and sun, but halfway through I would quite literally lose the thread, along with any interest in completing the task. From there I would just furiously twirl the white buttons, blanketing the screen with a mess of lines, loops, and knots. I ended up being totally frustrated.

That's how I felt at the ElderHome meetings. I couldn't get a coherent picture. The agendas were rarely presented in advance, which peeved me. People would wander in and out during the meetings, which further agitated me. In my business career up to that point, attendees were expected to arrive early to meetings and stay until they were over. At first I thought there was some reason for this blatant disregard of order and authority; our residents and patients were our priority, after all. One could never know when Mr. Thompson might fall, and the ops manager needed to be there to help document the incident. Or perhaps Mrs. Allessandro was moving in that day, and the ops manager needed to be on site to welcome the family and steer them toward her new apartment. I came to realize, however, that there were simply different rules for meetings when it came to healthcare organizations—at least the one I worked for.

Several people were repeatedly late or no-shows at our meetings, but Wendy, who generally chaired them, seemed unfazed by their absence, and there never appeared to be any repercussions. One of these individuals gave the impression her time was more important than everyone else's. Sometimes she would call in to the meetings from her "office," and I could hear her dog barking in the background. No one said a word. Her name was Vicky.

After largely ignoring me my first month of work, Vicky inexplicably offered to take me to lunch. It was an invitation I felt obliged to accept, and she both picked the place and drove. We were gone close to two hours. I got fidgety, knowing I was expected back at Stratford, but Vicky seemed oblivious. She just chatted away and prodded me with questions that made me uncomfortable. When she dropped me back at Stratford, she said she was going to spend the rest of the afternoon at the elite old-school athletic club we both belonged to on Portland's west side. Jay and I had moved on from the SAC, and the club was definitely a status symbol, with not just athletic offerings but also social ones. I myself would never have been so brazen as to leave work in the middle of the day to partake in its activities. Vicky smiled serenely and proffered a jazzy wave as she pulled away.

As I got to know Vicky better, I looked for ways to avoid her. She dressed like a 1950s schoolteacher in plaid skirts and sweater sets with pearls, all apparently newly purchased. Once, unable to avoid sitting next to her, I noticed a Nordstrom's tag still attached to her suit jacket. After that I paid closer attention to her attire and realized she rarely repeated the same outfit twice.

Vicky was neither thin nor fat, short nor tall. She was completely nondescript, the epitome of a lump. Her hair was a tangle of brown and gray, her attempts to tamp it down with various hairstyles unsuccessful. Her eyes were large and deceptively innocent; I learned too slowly they were not to be trusted.

On first meeting you, Vicky would broadly smile. She seemed full of questions but rarely added anything of merit to a discussion. Over time I began to question her general knowledge and experience and wondered how she had become an ops manager of one of our two day-only facilities. I overheard her saying she had obtained her master's in healthcare administration at a well-known school in the Portland area, but I found this hard to believe.

In fact, there was little that was believable about Vicky.

She struck me as someone pretending to be something they were not. She was like a chameleon. Her personality would change depending on the person she found herself talking to. With a younger, less experienced person, her posture would loosen and her language would become hipper. When she was with someone senior to her, though, she was suddenly as reserved and respectful as a schoolgirl, sitting upright in her chair and choosing her words carefully. Everything about her made my skin crawl.

I learned that she had a child, yet she never mentioned it, which also bothered me and fit with the self-interested and hollow character she represented and that I had begun to fear.

A few months later, when the new director of ElderHome decided this woman would replace Wendy as my boss, I privately renamed her "Icky."

14

A FAMILY SPLIT

My mother raised me to believe I could do anything if I wanted to. Weekday mornings I would climb under the down comforter in her still-warm bed and watch her as she "put on her face" at her Art Deco vanity table. Our house was full of furniture and pieces from the 1920s and 1930s, in part due to my parents' inheriting them and in part because they loved those designs and all things French.

My mother would perch in her satin slip on the vanity bench, applying creamy foundation to her cheeks and lavender eye shadow and black mascara around her hazel green eyes. She was a tall woman, and slim, with long, graceful fingers and narrow feet. She commanded your attention. I wanted to be just like her when I grew up, with a job, a company-issued car (a Ford Taurus replaced every two years), a travel budget, office holiday parties, and business cards, which she used haphazardly as reminder notes in the house, when no other paper could be found: "Josh, 6 p.m. parent-teacher conference," "Erin, peel the carrots and potatoes before 7."

The part I didn't want to copy was the person she became at home. The powerful woman striding through her work-day, full of confidence and expertise, returned home after 5 p.m., put down her purse, washed off her makeup, and gave in to grief over her relationship with my father. Their con-versations, once so passionate and full of private jokes, had dwindled to polite or indifferent exchanges regarding the need for more milk from the store, the weather, or a child's report card. I observed my father silently leaving the house after my mother arrived home. He'd go to smoke cigarettes with his friends down at the Veritable Quandary, a local watering hole, and have a beer or coffee. My mother made dinner for us; the sounds of her cooking echoed like cymbals throughout the house. We would sit at the table, and she would barely eat; then she'd change into her nightgown and wander off to bed before darkness had barely crept into the house.

My parents' divorce seemed to take my whole adolescent life, starting when I was twelve and my mother informed me that all was not well between them.

"I don't think we will stay married much longer, Erin," she said, pausing at a red light as we drove to the grocery store.

I looked at my mother. Divorce was still relatively uncom-mon in my peer group in 1980. I had no experience with how it played out. Hallie's parents had recently divorced. Her mother came to school to talk to our sixth-grade teacher about it, to explain in advance, in case Hallie started to act up, I suppose. I watched the three of them move into the hall, where Hallie burst into tears. It was the only time I ever saw her do that.

She was stoic after that. She'd pack her backpack every other weekend to sleep at her dad's new apartment. He was a photographer, and his second bathroom was a jungle of weird lights and trays filled with murky liquids and a clothesline strung with black-and-white photos of his three children. When Hallie was there, he would make her ravioli and put on Michael Jackson records, and they would dance until they couldn't stop laughing. He would listen as she talked about wanting to play music and sing for her career, and he didn't mind if she fell asleep on the couch watching movies like *The Exorcist*.

I don't recall if I asked my mother any questions after she told me about the rocky state of her marriage. Knowing her, I was sure everything would all come out eventually.

I loved my father, and I didn't want him to leave. I loved it when he made his "kitchen-sink" spaghetti sauce, simmering garlic, onions, sausages, and several cans of plum tomatoes for several hours on the stove. I loved the way he would take naps on the couch on Sundays, listening to Stan Getz or Dizzy Gillespie on the radio. My father never complained, even when my mother woke him from his dozing to go pick up one of us from gymnastics, ballet, basketball practice, or a party. I loved the way he tried to find ways to avoid arguing with my mother, when she really wanted to fight. I can count on one hand the number of times I saw him angry. He was kind, patient, and he loved words, like me.

My parents stayed together for another five years, more out of necessity than lack of imagination. Surely my mother would have left sooner, if she could have made the finances work. There was the fact of their friendship, too. Despite their difficulties, the bond between them was a strong knot. Still, the stress of their continuing to live together when their romantic love had dissipated wore on all of us like a relentless rain.

My mother started to work half the week in Seattle, a three-hour drive away, living in an apartment with my sister who spent half her days in tights and pointe shoes at dance practice. My father sunk into a depression, retreating from his teaching and spending more and more time at the Veritable Quandary or dozing on the couch. My brother and I both had school, sports, and a solid group of friends rescuing us, like lifeboats next to a sinking cruise liner. I nurtured my budding eating disorder and earnestly studied brochures from colleges for escape.

I also turned to spiritual undertakings, like tarot cards, divination, and a fascination with the occult. I placed a great deal of trust in astrology; it alleviated my anxiety to have some hope for the future. I became ritualistic about food as well, invoking tea ceremonies, exploring vegetarianism, and fasting.

Years later my siblings and I would often talk about those days, each adding colorful details from our unique experience. Josh had the gift of storytelling and could remember the breed of the dog someone brought to a spontaneous high school party at our house when our parents had taken a rare weekend away. Caitlin listened, smiling slightly and stretching her long, ballet dancer legs, while I bubbled with laughter.

"They had gone to Carmel," I interjected as Josh framed the scene. "A last attempt to salvage their marriage." Caitlin looked at me and frowned, her dark eyebrows tenting.

"I don't remember that."

"That's because you were in Seattle, dancing. I think you may have come home for the weekend. But you didn't know all that was going on with them." In retrospect I found that odd. My mother lived with my sister in Seattle two or three days a week. What did they talk about? I pictured my sister with sore feet, bundled in sweatpants and hand-knit leg warmers, watching *The Golden Girls* on a small television, while my mother prepared pasta for their dinner.

Josh continued. "And then, Mickey Smalls . . . Remember him? Mickey had a giant round head and bushy red hair. He could find weed within half an hour if you asked. Never revealed his source, which you know, pissed me off at the time. But I kind of understand it now. He was a businessman."

"Mickey was the one who got the dog high," I said. I remember how uncomfortable that made me, at age fifteen. Who gets an animal high? Beer and pot flowed freely at the party. And Mickey purposely blew bong smoke in the dog's face. She was a golden retriever, and ten minutes later she hadn't moved from where she was blocking the hallway. I remember pulling her by her collar into a quiet corner of the living room.

"You were always the prude," Josh said, not unkindly. My brother accepted people at face value. He was comfortable with chaos, with messiness, with people spoiling for a fight.

Nothing made him uneasy. He didn't like being told what to do, though. If there was something you needed from him, you had to make it seem as if it was his idea.

I knew he loved me for the differences between us—my "preppiness" and my ambition. Josh had more friends than anyone I knew or have known since. Kids came in hordes to that impromptu party. Josh was only fourteen, but most of them were his friends, his personal tribe.

Josh played keyboards in a band, and the group started up in the basement sometime after eleven. Josh bent over his instrument, as girls watched him covetously from the shadows. Caitlin was upstairs with her boyfriend in our room. Hallie and I and another friend of ours grabbed a beer and headed toward the playground of the grade school down the street. A crescent moon was up, and stars dappled the dark sky like kosher salt. I had a pack of clove cigarettes, and we drank our beers and artfully blew smoke rings into the night.

By the time the letter from Brown came, admitting me to the class of 1990, my mother had left the family, but as far as I knew, my parents were still married. Our home no longer felt like a home to me but more like a waiting room in a train station. We went about our business like strangers holding tickets to different destinations, making room on the couch to free up a seat for one another. We sipped weak coffee, read pages from the daily newspaper, and kept conversations to safe subjects, such as what shoes to wear to the prom, whether the Oregon salmon were going to be producing this year, and what did one think of the new host on the late-night show?

I left for Providence, Rhode Island, on a warm Portland day in August, a few boxes of books sent ahead of me on a UPS truck, my suitcase packed to the brim, and a sturdy backpack slung over my shoulders. My father dropped me off at the airport and gave me a hug.

"I am so proud of you, Erin. Knock 'em dead! Ivy League! That's my daughter." He kissed me, and I walked away, then looked back to see him smiling and waving from the old Toyota, the bright sun glancing off his mirrored sunglasses.

My parents divorced while I was away. My mother moved to Australia to pursue a newfound love and left my father to deal with the matter of the house, which was still partially unfinished. For a year he remained unsure and morose, apparently unable to cope. He had relied on my mother for so long. My sister was then in Eugene, working and studying journalism at the university. My brother was still in high school, and eventually he and my father finished what they could, painting, mopping, unrolling rugs, and so forth. The house sold with little fanfare to a couple with visions of what could be. My father moved into a condo downtown, and my brother left to attend college in Las Vegas on a soccer scholarship. I was in Providence, trying bravely to face my new life.

15

MY MOTHER, THE EXPAT

When my mother was fifty, she moved to Australia. She'd met her new partner, Maurey, the previous year, when she was on vacation with a friend. He was seventeen years her junior but looked five years older. She transferred to the Australian office of her company, and together she and Maurey bought a one-level house off a narrow street in a suburb of Sydney, with a sun-dappled backyard covered in moss and slate tiles, a eucalyptus tree in one corner, and a chimenea in the other. Their furniture was sparse, as though they were young new-lyweds just getting started in life.

Maurey was gritty, while my mother was refined. He'd scoop her up by her waist for a goodbye kiss as he headed to work in his striped, short-sleeved button-down with his name embroidered across the left pocket where his smokes bulged from their permanent spot. Most evenings he would grill bangers or lamb chops on the barbie, and then he'd hit the pub with his mates while my mother made her long commute home from her office across the city, navigating tricky road signs and deftly driving on the left side of the yellow center line.

Stylish as always, my mother kept her hair coiffed, her sandals strappy, and her linen pants without a crease. She was pert and full of life, enamored of her new city, basking in her newfound love, in reinventing herself after slamming the door on the life that had been my father, my sister, my brother, and me.

I was not raised to question my mother's choices. She made them, and we all adapted. She was good at making choices, after all. My father was more of a follower and for a number of years had no troubles existing in the world my mother chose for us. But gradually his spirit slipped away. It took a long time before he could figure out what to do next.

For me in Providence, when I thought of home, I imagined it like an empty boathouse with pilings where each of our boats had been tied covered with moss, and with bits of rope and abandoned floats still tethered to the dock. Looking out from there, one could envision the moonlight like a walkway across the water, illuminating the course each of our boats had taken.

I was not angry at my mother for leaving. I was just lost. I was also terrified, having gone the opposite direction geographically, to an Ivy League college on the East Coast. Everything was different in Providence—the people, their clothing, their way of speaking, the musty smell of old build-ings and radiator heat, and the color of the fall leaves. I was afraid of my professors, afraid of the coming winter, afraid of eating a fish called "scrod," afraid of living with my new roommate, and afraid of failing my courses. And I was sad, eating everything I could get my hands on, but mostly bags of peanut M&M's. I missed my mother terribly, and she was halfway across the world.

Meanwhile I had to find ways to make money while juggling my challenging studies. I worked in the cafeteria and the library. I took odd jobs babysitting and housecleaning for professors and families who lived near campus. I worked weekends at the campus liquor store, selling cases of beer, bourbon, and Oregon pinot noir to students and retired people alike, cautioned by the owner to card anyone who looked under thirty. I never wanted to have to manage my finances as my mother had, counting money to the penny and being forced to choose between soccer cleats for one child or ballet slippers for the other, between turning the baseboard heat on or lighting the woodstove.

I was determined not to end up poor, so I ignored all thoughts of pursuing a creative career. I wanted to be a writer, but I had my father as an example; he was a writer with graduate school loans, and though he published a few times, he could barely pay the rent before meeting my mother. I would not be that person struggling to make it, staying up until 3 a.m. with a cheap bottle of wine by my side, a naked bulb flickering overhead, and a lumpy futon and hot plate in the corner.

While I was at college, I moved from dorm to dorm, never bothering to return home to visit after the summer of my freshman year. Instead, during school breaks I would accompany my friends home to Cape Cod, Connecticut, or Florida. My friends' parents were educated and had deep pockets. They were gracious hosts with homes casually appointed with furniture, knickknacks, books, and tableware passed down through generations.

Sometimes I would stay in Providence and sublet a room from a friend whose belongings were sparse and manageable; I would simply move them to the side and throw down my own futon and comforter. With other subletting friends, I would cook Indian food in old kitchens chock-full of mottled pots, pans, and spatulas, leaving doors open to let in the humid air.

By my sophomore year my classmates were planning for their junior year abroad. I was bored and at my most unhappy. My eating disorder was at its peak, as was my weight. I was a resident counselor on a freshman hall and would drown my misery in shots of Jim Beam on Saturday nights, occasionally adding greasy pizza from the snack bar that was open until 2 a.m. I lacked the conviction that being at an Ivy league school, reading and writing about the classics, and traipsing past piles of orange and scarlet leaves on the college green was the answer to my existence.

I decided I would not go the pedestrian route my junior year. No, I would go to Africa. *French-speaking Africa.* I would put the French language classes I had taken since age six and the French literature classes I was immersed in at Brown to the test. I would place myself somewhere so far away, so beyond these ivory-tower walls that no one would know me when I got back.

I persisted in fantasies of being completely transformed by an African year abroad, losing weight by subsisting on stew with white rice and cassava leaves. Brown did not have any program that fit with this study-abroad fantasy, but I found one through Kalamazoo College that would let me attend Fourah Bay College in Sierra Leone. I met with the study-abroad counselor, who looked at the research I had done and gently advised it "might be difficult" to achieve, given my "financial aid status." She pulled a thin folder of paperwork for Brown's own semester-long program in Lyon, France, from a stack on her desk.

"Here," she said, tapping precisely in the center of the top brochure. "I suggest you fill out this application so you have a backup, just in case you can't quite get the registrar *slash* financial aid office to get on board with your plan."

I was annoyed with her from the moment she pushed the folder in my direction, but my irritation inched up measurably with her use of the word "slash." I swept up the materials (our allotted fifteen minutes had passed) about a study-abroad program that reeked of the mundane, and held my head high as I left her office. Outside, four other students occupied the hard wooden chairs lined up by her door. I could feel eager eyes on my back as I walked toward the stairwell. I knew what they were thinking: *I wonder where she is planning to go.*

Six months later, I found myself on the plane with a friend named Amy, on my way to Lyon, with a few weeks first in

Paris to acclimate to France. I submerged my disappointment by gorging on a hunk of brie spread on a generous loaf of French bread.

In France I managed to live for six months off a meager $1,000 in savings. While my well-heeled classmates from Brown left every weekend, using their train passes to explore other exotic European cities, I stayed in Lyon and walked the narrow streets, inhaling the aroma of *pain aux raisins* emanating from every corner boulangerie. I lived off rice, eggs, bread, and cheese, and the occasional bottle of red table wine. I grew fatter and covered myself in a man's wool coat that I found in a thrift shop and bought for ten dollars. I attended classes at the university and struggled to follow the professors' lectures, answer the questions on the final exam, and fulfill the requirement to write a paper, in French.

My memories of that time are spotty; my unhappiness was profound. I tried to ignore the man who masturbated in the public park we passed on our way to class in the mornings, though once Lisa, a petite girl from Florida, picked up a rock and threw it at him. It landed near his right foot, and he gaped at her as he pulled up his pants.

There were some pleasurable times, too, like the Thanksgiving meal a group of us Americans prepared. Lisa challenged me to tequila shots, and after six of them I fell backward into my friend Jake's arms. There were the weekends Jake would stay at my apartment and play his guitar shirtless in my bed. He'd smooth my hair before I slept but never kissed me.

There were so many walks in so many parks with so many little dogs and stylish French women wearing scarves at their throats and leather pumps on their feet.

There was the swing dancing in a bar where the French men took all of us girls into their arms and spun us, spun us, spun us until we were a dizzy, giggling mess.

There was a wild night in an apartment in Paris toward Christmas before we all headed home. The party at a friend of a friend's had all kinds of couples hooking up and went on until the wine ran out, there was nothing to eat, and we all fell into a somnolent heap on the floor.

When I returned to Brown, I was transformed, but I didn't know it yet. I had cast aside the version of myself that felt I would never be loved, and I had explored avenues in my heart where I had previously refused to go. I had tussled in bed with men I would once have ignored. I had started seeking out pleasure and worrying less about what I looked like with my clothes off, or whether there would be something to say the next day. It was shocking that I could be so blithely indifferent and feel glorious at the same time.

Back in Providence, halfway through my senior year, I realized I had learned how to be at college on the East Coast. I was, in fact, an *East Coaster*. On the phone my sister had to tell me to slow down because she couldn't follow my rapid speech. I had fantastic friends—young men and women who studied hard like me, who came from families with their own dysfunctions, and who had their own insecurities and fears. We banded together and protected each

other and found ways to laugh, to see the days into evenings, the evenings into weekends, and the weekends into
semester breaks. When I went home with them on holidays
and long weekends, I could see the drama in their lives, and
I relished being on the outside looking in.

One or two of my friends had such seemingly happy and
well-balanced home lives that I couldn't help looking for
cracks in the utopia: Was that a sour look on her mother's
face? Isn't a cluttered study evidence of mental illness? Did
I hear loud voices in the middle of the night as I slept in the
guest room on unfamiliar sheets?

I was mentally jotting down everything about the people
I lived among and those they introduced me to. It was a rare
time in my life when I got to observe the private family lives
of others. As we become adults we're privy to friends' interior lives less and less. Visits to their homes become more of
a show-and-tell, less authentic. Before the guests arrive we
put our dirty dishes away, we vacuum, and we cut the lawn.

Some of my dearest college friends came from a lot of
wealth; others were just like me, dependent on financial aid
or student loans. But, dammit, we were united in the fact
that we were all at Brown. We may have felt alone when we
arrived, but we were not alone by the time we left.

As I look back, I realize that I had found a new family at
college. Then when I met Scott, soon after I turned twenty-one, his attentions to me seemed to heal the wounds that
festered with the loss of my Portland home. Scott was there
to help make a new family of my very own.

16

DOCTORS AND NURSES

My college years were fraught with eating disorders until I returned from France, when I decided to start loving myself enough to take ownership of my own body. I was reminded of that at Stratford, where I witnessed the residents struggling with their bodies, at an advanced age, and it pained me. For many of them the issues were more than just aging, or obesity. There was lung cancer, lupus, AIDS, melanoma, hypertension, angina, stroke, edema, heart issues, liver failure, all varieties of addiction, mental illness, phobias, delirium, urinary tract infections, common colds and flu, and dementia. We were, after all, an ALF, with an on-site medical clinic staffed by a doctor and two primary nurses. There was intentional separation between the nurses on the floor of the residents' building and those who worked in the clinic. The difference included status, as well as licensing overseen by the state. This didn't matter to the residents, however, who would stop any of the nurses in the hall to request a blood-pressure reading, a dose of their meds, or a *Reader's Digest* assessment of whatever currently ailed them.

A fireproof metal door separated the clinic from the housing. After the grand opening of the clinic, the door was generally open during the day. Josie, the clinic receptionist, sat at a round desk behind windows that slid open so she could greet patients. Residents would drift in and out of the reception area, chatting Josie up, lounging for hours in the chairs. They might not necessarily have an appointment, but the clinic was new and the chairs accommodating. Josie was friendly and kind. I had to remind her to advise the casual visitors that she had work to do.

After a while too many residents came to the clinic without an appointment. Josie or the clinic nurse, Sarah, constantly had to question those who walked in.

"Good morning, Annie," Sarah might say. "Do you have an appointment today?"

Annie looked at her as she leaned on her walker, befuddled. "Why, no, I don't believe so. Maybe it's next week?" Her knotted hands pointed toward Josie.

"Let's check, shall we?" Sarah smiled and asked Josie to look at her appointment schedule. Josie peered out at Annie and advised her it was next week.

"Two p.m. next Thursday, Miss Annie! The doctor will see you then." Annie nodded and sighed, turning slowly to head back through the clinic door.

We had to start closing the door, which left Josie feeling as if she were locked in. I knew she didn't care for it, but at least she could look out the window onto the main thoroughfare with its daily activity. Meanwhile the residents would cluster outside the closed clinic door, forming some semblance of a line with their personal mobility devices and their walkers. Some brought their own chairs to sit on. The staff and I would periodically move them along, like protestors outside a workplace. I imagined what their signs would have said.

"Can you help me?"

"I don't feel very good."

"I just want someone to look me in the eye."

The clinic had a different atmosphere than the ALF, more professional, with stricter regulations. It was less chaotic in the clinic, and I would sometimes wander down there just to chat with Josie, social worker Lydia, or the doctor who came in three days a week.

Hiring the doctor and a director of nursing (who oversaw the nurses in the ALF and the clinic) was as challenging as everything else at Stratford. To fill in, nurses from other ElderHome residences were brought in on a rotating basis to manage the nursing staff. It was nothing short of mayhem and clear that most of these interim nurses couldn't wait to get back to the quiet routine of our sister facilities where they officially worked.

As part of my orientation I had visited each of the other facilities, and Wendy held our ops managers' meetings at a different building each month. Each had its own personality. One might be described as "low census" or "high dementia" (translation: "quiet"). Another might be called an "energetic community" (meaning "active, least amount of interventions needed, most profitable"). And then there was "challenging" Stratford, with "extensive needs" and "high turnover" (as Wendy said, "a hot mess").

ElderHome's senior director of nursing interviewed a handful of nurses for the post at Stratford. She was not impressed. Community nursing draws a special breed of nurses, often unusual types who share a common desire to help people down on their luck. They might be interested in social justice or they might just be extroverts who, being messy themselves, are not put off by the messiness of other people and their lives. They may be smart enough to get through nursing school but are not necessarily intellectual or sophisticated. Some of the nurses I met were downright wacky, with badly dyed hair; poorly applied mascara; pigeons or parakeets as pets; handbags teeming with movie stubs, gum, peanuts, and drugstore receipts; and an unbridled enthusiasm for discussing people's bowel movements.

We finally found someone who had taught at a local nursing school, had traveled to Ghana and India, where she had volunteered as a nurse to those in need, and who owned a home near Stratford. She was an aging hippie and truly brilliant. I liked Myrna, in part because her mothering instinct was fierce. She spoke exuberantly and loud, and if she was eating while she talked, food often flew from her mouth. I learned to keep my distance when we were together at lunch.

Myrna encouraged me; on days when I questioned whether I could go on, she would remind me how tough I was, and who the bad guys were, and how it was best to just take things one step at a time. Myrna, Patty (the activities coordinator), and I formed a support group of sorts, meeting on occasion at Myrna's house for wine and cheese after work.

"Vicky is an IDIOT!" Myrna said, spewing a little merlot mixed with Roquefort toward Patty. Patty spread some brie on a cracker and threw back her head laughing.

"I know," she said. "I could NOT BELIEVE what she said to Mr. Rotwein." She was referring to a resident who had asked Vicky if he could have meals delivered to his room because he couldn't tolerate the mean people in the dining room.

Vicky had looked at him and said, "Is there something wrong with you, Mr. Rotwein, that EVERYONE in the dining room wants to be mean to you, and you alone?" She could be intolerably cruel to residents that way.

"It's like she was trying to egg him on!" said Patty.

I looked at both of them and smiled for the first time in several weeks, realizing that I had finally made friends at work. That was always one of the questions in the employee polls I'd taken at other jobs, along with ones about your boss's leadership skills, whether you felt empowered to make decisions, and if you were receiving the training you needed. I had not received a survey yet from ElderHome about my current role (and I couldn't wait!), but at least there was one question I could answer with "yes."

It took six months to find a doctor for the Stratford clinic. Dr. Goodsmith was tall, soft-spoken, and dignified. She was welcomed with open arms and hearty applause at the first care meeting she attended. That was where the leaders at Stratford—clinic nurse, director of nursing, doctor, social worker, ops manager, and so on—would discuss our most complex cases and strategize what more we could do for them with the limited resources available to us.

Three months later Dr. Goodsmith handed me her letter of resignation as we sat at the round table in my office. She had folded the note and placed it in an envelope with my full name carefully written in her beautiful cursive. After I read it, she told me, her voice trembling, that the problem wasn't me.

"I have enjoyed working with you, Erin," she said. "I have just decided to move back home. I don't think Portland is where I want to be." Home for her was a small town in Virginia. She was older than me and had a grown son. She didn't talk about him much. I felt her loneliness like a cold draft, whenever she entered a room. I pictured her packing boxes in her apartment, labeling them "medical textbooks," "winter sweaters," and "Opera CDs."

I wondered why this kind of action was possible for her but not me. To just get up from your chair and decide to leave. I knew she had been appalled by how sick the Stratford residents were. I knew she had come from treating the elderly in a hospital system where there was a daily routine, where patients came and left and perhaps never came back again. Where she could go get a cup of tea and find a quiet corner in the hospital's cafeteria during her break. Where the bathrooms were clean and the floors sparkly. Where staff reported to work and weren't dysfunctional. Where she could just be a doctor and not something more.

Vicky had publicly admonished Dr. Goodsmith just two days earlier for showing up late for meetings, pointing out that everyone had to deal with unexpected traffic delays and she should plan accordingly. Vicky, who was regularly late for meetings when she made them at all, spouted this with the fierce rigidity of a Catholic school headmistress. The timing of the doctor's resignation was not lost on me; the rebuke was likely what tipped the scales.

After Dr. Goodsmith left, my despondency grew. Would we ever have a fully functioning clinic with our own doctor on site? I was naïvely hoping that the clinic would somehow save everything that was wrong with Stratford. That it would bring that element of order that the building so needed, like the first general store in an old western town. But there was a complete lack of interest in the position, and the residents continued to be bussed by ElderHome to their physicians throughout the city. Those who had switched to Dr. Goodsmith were understandably irritated by her departure. It was not easy to return to their previous physicians, since many were no longer taking new patients. The doctors' limited bucket for Medicaid patients was full. I worried, too, that the longer we went without a doctor, the less likely it was that residents would make the switch back once we found one. And without the clinic income, we would continue to operate at a significant loss.

Enter Dr. Swidwell.

Dr. Swidwell looked like an oversize elf. He could have easily worn a pair of green stockings and red knickers to the clinic, and no one would have found it strange. He had a baritone laugh that germinated in his intestines and barreled out of his lungs. I liked him instantly. He wore chinos held up by a canvas belt, and unremarkable leather shoes, and he always placed his warm hand on a patient's shoulder in compassion. His presence gave the clinic a healthy glow. It was true he had come out of retirement to take the position, which was only part-time, but with the numbers of residents we had, a part-time doctor was all that we needed.

Dr. Swidwell had been working in geriatrics for most of his career and was now a senior citizen himself. When he first retired, he advised me one afternoon over tea in my office, he felt like a man standing in the middle of a bridge, trying to decide how to cross.

"I said to Paul, my partner, Paul, who can always see through the clouds of uncertainty I am apt to create over nothing at all . . . I said, 'Paul, I am a man on this bridge, and from one end is the youthful man and physician I once was, the cocky gent, the know-it-all telling folks to stop doing this and that and start doing this or that and your health will improve and you won't be falling and you'll stave off cancer and heart disease and so forth. On the other end is this aging man, me, Paul, me in *retirement*, the man you wake up to each morning and bring espresso and an orange, the man who never bothered to practice what he preached—jogging, a vegan diet, more sleep. But in truth, I am that man on the bridge in the middle, looking fondly down on the schools of fish puckering up for some crumbs, wondering if it's time to go fishing or just feed them, to feed or be fed.'"

I was mostly following Dr. Swidwell's metaphor, and my nod was all he needed to forge on.

"So, of course, Paul, being Paul, swept aside the mystery of it all and sat me down at the table and poured me a nip of brandy, and you know what he said, Erin? After all that, my heart bent inside out and raw and exposed, which of course he has seen before, but it's still novel every time, just how smart he is, how well he knows me. He said, 'My darling Doc, it sounds like you already know what you are after here.' And he was right. I was six months into retirement, and I was just staring over the middle of that bridge like a troubled person considering jumping. Trust me I was not!"

He patted me on the shoulder.

"I threw back that brandy," he went on, "and with great drama slammed it on the table!" Dr. Swidwell demonstrated with a smack of his palm on the table between us. I only jumped slightly, caught up as I was with his story and the relationship he had with Paul.

"You're right, Paul, of course you are. You just always are. I want to return to work, maybe not full-time, but I need to be with my patients again. I need to not be that man aging in the painting, observing from afar."

I guessed he was referring to *The Picture of Dorian Gray*,

and I intuited that the good doctor was telling me he was like the rest of the residents, that he was *one* of them. It was perhaps this that drew me to Dr. Swidwell. His compassion was uniquely his own, with human imperfections and uncertainty mixed in, as real as his curly gray hair.

17

THE CONTRACTOR

My first husband, Scott, was a contractor. He specialized in kitchens and bathrooms, and his work was solid, his clients happy with his professional demeanor and his use of quality products with sustainable designs. We had met the summer before my senior year at Brown. He attended Johnson & Wales, a career-oriented school that didn't require SAT scores and was a good three- to four-hour drive from his parents' house in New Jersey. When he left for college, Scott told me later, he had simply packed his sapphire blue Camaro with a few choice belongings and headed north, thinking that maybe he'd meet someone like me.

On my first date with Scott, we went through the McDonald's drive-through; I ordered french fries and he got coffee. He told me about his ambitions to run his own business, to invest in the stock market, to one day own a house at the Jersey Shore. I was charmed by his vigor and his certainty that the world would give him what he knew it could. In that moment, I knew that Scott and I shared a common belief we could be economically successful with hard work and keen minds. That shared ambition drove us headlong into our relationship with dreams of an abundant future within our grasp.

He wooed me with country breakfasts cooked in his kitchen, flowers on my doorstep, and weekend trips to the shore. Our relationship was passionate and full of abandon. Yet I felt at times as if we had chosen each other so we could play house, like two children with child-size brooms and lawn mowers. We were ready to discard the shells of childhoods that had turned sour, and we believed, with all the fervor of young lovers lying hand and hand on the beach, that we could make a better life for ourselves and for our future children.

The abundant sex was new to me, and I relished it, amazed that someone would want my body next to theirs and so frequently. Happily I swam a mile at the Brown pool almost every day, lived off a bagel or two, fruit, and coffee, and lost thirty pounds by the time classes commenced in the fall.

I was new to the idea of a long-term relationship, and I worked hard at maintaining ours, despite the differences between us. Scott struggled with his calculus class and was pursuing a business degree, while I was on a full scholarship, majoring in comparative literature and French. He was from a conservative small town; his family had awkward social skills and harbored myriad secrets. I was from Portland, Oregon, which had always drawn nonconformists, entrepreneurs, and people trying to find themselves. My family may have disintegrated, but underneath it all we were tied together by a current of love. Somehow I knew we would find our way back to one another eventually, while it seemed Scott preferred to distance himself from his family, finding himself the black sheep, so different from them.

Over time I recognized other differences between us. Some were small, simple things, such as how he took his coffee (cream and sugar, while I liked milk; though later I convinced him to drop the sugar) and how I exercised almost daily while he watched television with a large bag of tortilla chips at his side. Other things were more serious—the way he spoke to his mother on the phone and, worse, how he spoke about her the rest of the time.

I returned to Portland after graduation, and Scott soon suggested I fly back east so we could drive cross-country together. He was ready for a new adventure, and I was helpless to stop him. I had not said no, but I also had not shouted a resounding yes either. I had felt fat and unhappy with most things when Scott and I met that hot summer in Providence, and in his desire for me, I had found some salvation.

Married life seemed inevitable once we were living together. Also a yearning for children had taken hold of me, and Scott and I now had a history to which I was loyal. I was sure I would never find someone else, that I was being overly picky, and surely all love relationships were hard to maintain. With much trepidation, I married Scott four years after we met, when I was twenty-five and he twenty-six. My mother flew in from Sydney with Maurey and her eleven-year-old stepdaughter.

Settled in Portland, I launched myself into my new job as a legal assistant for Systran, a factoring company that bought freight bills from truckers for seventy-five cents on the dollar. Scott started building a local clientele for his remodeling business, and we rented a cheap one-bedroom apartment in Southwest Portland with a stream passing by below our deck and a cloak of sorrowful-looking trees. Always dank, the apartment smelled of mud and crushed leaves. We later moved to Lake Oswego, where the view from our large front window revealed an expanse of green lawn to the railroad tracks and, beyond, the syrupy lake. It was like living in a Renoir painting.

We were young and happily ignored anything that didn't align between us. Our hormones prevailed for a good long while. As it turned out, I had a lot to learn about love and had not chosen well. Over time, the differences between us became more apparent, and I found myself internally covering for what I viewed as Scott's deficiencies (as a husband, as a father, and as a person) more and more, until I was nearly blind with the effort of explaining to myself what he really meant to say, what he really meant to do, and what he actually believed.

The storm clouds were evident in the bouts of anger from Scott if I spoke the wrong words or demanded too much from him. I started to learn his triggers and adjusted accordingly, but every few months something new would set him off. He'd slam the door as hard as he could, heading for his truck, and I would find myself alone in the apartment.

Scott easily found work from the well-off people in the neighborhood. He was affable and observant, and at the local diner, he would strike up a conversation, eventually shifting the talk to windows that needed replacing, floors needing sanding, or bathrooms stuck in the 1950s.

I worked equally hard to learn about factoring and the trucking industry. My income and responsibility expanded quickly, and soon I was working long hours at the office, running for miles on the weekends, and experimenting with cooking in our kitchen. When Scott bought me a KitchenAid mixer and a bathrobe, I tried not to grimace; they conjured up images of his mother in her primrose-patterned robe in her kitchen in New Jersey, a Marlboro 100 perched delicately between her manicured fingers as she spoke in her vague, slightly movie-starlet way.

We bought our first house after much searching for the right fixer-upper in what we believed was an up-and-coming neighborhood. Portland was growing fast, and real estate was booming. Scott decided we should start buying houses to flip them or keep as rentals. My income was essential for this, because Scott was a sole proprietor, and banks didn't look fondly at the self-employed when doling out mortgages.

The 1970s split-level ranch house was not one I ever imagined owning. I had grown up dreaming of stone country houses in Provence, four-square-style homes with dormers and large front porches in Portland, and three-story turn-of-the-century brick townhomes on tree-lined Brooklyn streets.

This place was a disaster; it had single-paned, anodized

aluminum-framed windows throughout and a kitchen with mud-brown cabinets, oppressive soffits, and harvest-colored appliances. The smell of cat urine was trapped in the brown-and-yellow shag carpet.

When my childhood fears of remodeling resurfaced, Scott quieted them, cuddling me on his lap and petting my hair. "It's going to be different this time, honey. Trust me," he said. "I get the job done."

He turned his attention to the most glaring offenses first and worked so avidly at replacing the windows, ripping up the carpet, tearing down the wall between the kitchen and living room, laying new hardware floors, and creating a new great room and kitchen that I hardly even noticed the flurry of activity, sheetrock, hammers, and dust. For my husband's vision and work ethic, I was grateful.

His best friend, Bill, arrived from New Jersey to help, and we set him up in one of the four bedrooms. At the end of the day the two men would tear into the plates of spaghetti I served up with garlic bread and red table wine, their conversation full of the hard labor of the day.

I was running even more then with a girlfriend, perhaps to limit the hours before bed after I returned home at night. I realized I was not at my best with a visitor living with us and the disruption caused by the remodel. But when I surveyed the scene, I decided that things were okay. Scott had proven he could finish the projects he started, our marriage was on solid ground, and we had money. My income was more than my parents had ever made together. Thinking about it this way gave me a feeling of safety, like a life jacket keeping me afloat. Though Scott's income was intermittent—he was spending more hours on our house and less on projects he was being paid for—I trusted in his plan of sweat equals equity. I felt, perhaps a little uneasily, that everything would work out.

I decided it was time to get pregnant, and Scott amiably agreed. And like that, it happened, two months later. Bill had returned to New Jersey, and the house was resting from its recent facelift. There was just one other project I was keen on Scott's completing before our child arrived the following May. But he had signed on to several large-scale projects in Lake Oswego, and most evenings he just sank into his leather easy chair in front of the television.

"I promise, Erin, I will get the main bathroom done before the baby comes," he said, when *Seinfeld* went to the commercial break.

"It's just that I want to be able to give the baby a bath," I murmured. We had only showers in the two bathrooms in the house. I was tired and slightly nauseous all the time in that first trimester, stuffing my mouth full of crackers in a vain attempt to not throw up.

"I know, don't worry, Pooker," he said, using his nickname for me fondly. He pulled me into his lap, though his eyes never left the television screen.

I was eight months pregnant when I passed the bathroom in question for the two hundredth time, the bathroom that had not been touched. The toilet ran incessantly, the rust stain in the sink glared at me, and the cracked tiles in the shower seemed to widen before my eyes. Every time I brought up the bathroom, Scott evaded my questions and just kept reminding me he had promised to take care of it.

I started to lie awake at night with worry. The mind of a very pregnant woman is as frightening as a carnival's house of horrors. I was scared that we couldn't afford a baby. I was scared to give birth. I was scared I might die. I was scared there would be something wrong with the baby. I was scared that I did not love Scott anymore, and yet I was having our baby. I did not want him to touch me. I wanted him to finish the bathroom. I tried to breathe, but each day that came closer to my delivery seemed to intensify my fears.

Two weeks before the baby was due, I came home to find Scott in the bathroom with a crowbar, plastic laid carefully in the hall to capture the dust. I burst into tears and hid in our room. I did not want him to know the relief that had come surging into my veins. The baby and I could have a bath, after all.

18

DARLA

Not long after I started at Stratford, I inherited Darla, much like the young and inexperienced teacher in a school is assigned the most difficult and unmanageable student. The student who has already driven the most dedicated faculty members to tears and the less dedicated to shouting in the classroom. The first hint that I should expect a challenging new resident came in an operations managers' meeting at the head office. Darla was on the agenda, along with two or three other individuals in the ElderHome program who required discussion that day.

Wendy scribbled furiously on her agenda, taking notes as she led the meeting, crossing items off when a decision had been reached. A hush filled the room when she reached Darla's name. Several sets of eyes exchanged glances (but studiously avoided me), and Wendy looked pointedly at the ElderHome placement director, Ariel, who just played with her bouncy curls and adjusted her cat's-eye glasses on her nose.

"Ariel, would you like to lead the discussion on Darla for us?" Wendy smiled broadly, but her eyes flashed like warning signs. This look, I had come to understand, preceded her lack of patience with someone and was usually followed by a concrete directive that she would not tolerate any noodling around. I enjoyed this spectacle whenever I witnessed it, because in truth, just about everything discussed in these meetings led nowhere. Despite the mission-driven earnest souls in the room, there was general ineptitude in conducting a business meeting. The social workers especially seemed to be incapable of accomplishing set goals. They lacked any kind of business sense and repeatedly got mired in emotions. Ariel was the most experienced and likely the highest paid of the social workers, but her style, which included cheerleader hand gestures and spurts of unprofessional giggles, was not one I warmed to. I just wanted her to get to the point.

On the other hand, the social worker assigned to Stratford had garnered my deepest respect. Lydia was unique. She appeared younger than her years by a decade, had flawless skin, and dressed in loose-fitting Punjabi pants and tops woven from hemp or other organic fibers. She wore handmade necklaces with healing crystals. Her dark auburn hair flowed down her back like a horse's mane, lush and gleaming.

She had the capacity to instinctively read and care for the natures and needs of others, yet she could set definite boundaries. She did not carry their burdens with her and instead found joy and humor in every situation. Lydia was able to spend most of her day working with the residents and then leave everything behind at her desk, floating out the front door unruffled. I so wanted to emulate her.

Lydia, however, was not there discussing Darla.

Ariel looked at Wendy, giggled nervously, and then chirped, "Ah, yes, Darla!" She tugged at a curl and grimaced. "Well, you see, Darla is no longer happy at Charles Dickey's Place." There was a collective sigh around the room. A couple of ops managers nodded in acknowledgment.

"She's been there about a year," Ariel went on. "All seemed to be going well for a while, but she has recently developed a dislike of the administrator, she is frustrated by the lack of art supplies, she insists the cook is adding calories to her food, because she's gained weight, and despite several efforts at intervention, she remains unappeased."

Charles Dickey's Place was not under the ElderHome umbrella, but there were residents at other assisted living facilities in the area who attended day centers operated by ElderHome, where they could participate in activities and have their medical needs addressed. It seemed that Darla was one of them, and I knew that it was our preference to have such participants actually reside in our owned and operated residential buildings.

"Darla has requested that she move into Stratford."

All eyes, including Ariel's, were now looking at me. Detecting the tone of alarm, I remained still, waiting for additional details to be offered up. There was always more to the story I had found with this group, and everyone in these meetings liked to give their two cents. Wendy rolled her eyes.

"What reason has she given?" she snapped at Ariel.

Ariel responded with a rushed stream of words. "She

heard it was recently remodeled and under new management. That all sounded nice to her. And it's a large building. She wants more people to socialize with and more staff to help her with her needs."

Frank, the facilities director, glanced over at me. His eyes, surrounded by crinkly lines, were kind.

"So we just basically agree to move her every year?" he asked. "This would be the third time in as many years. She is not an easy person to move, as you all know, and there is no assurance she'll be any happier at Stratford than she was at any of the other places."

A wave of nods.

"Well, we *are* trying to grow census at Stratford, Frank," Ariel remarked petulantly. "And in case you haven't noticed, we haven't had a lot of takers."

This was true. One of the most time-consuming aspects of my job, along with the fruitless meetings and penning responses to grievances, was providing tours of the facility, the medical clinic, and a model apartment, after which I would sit and answer any questions from the proposed resident and their family, offer them a cup of tea, and hand them a small mountain of paperwork. This one- to two-hour process resulted in an actual interested party who also met our criteria for residency approximately one time out of eight.

Because tours were not always prearranged, I often found myself scrambling to find an empty apartment that was intact, clean, and ready for viewing. Each time a resident moved out, there was an extensive punch list of work needed to turn it over. Holes in the walls, mysterious stains on the carpet, malfunctioning toilets, and broken air-conditioning units were ubiquitous. Pam and Rhonda were in charge of maintaining the list of available one bedrooms and studios, with notations about their condition. After a few unfortunate tours, where I peeked in the apartment after unlocking the door and had to do a rapid 180-degree turn, advising the visitors at my heels that I must have written the number down wrong, I learned not to rely on the "ready list" posted in my office weekly. It was better to first ask Pam or Rhonda which room might be a good one to show and then take a quick tour of it myself.

Pam, who always seemed to be moving, manhandling a broom, a mop, or cleaning supplies like some added appendage, was generally full of details: "Definitely 406. I was just in there yesterday, cleaned it up real good. Mrs. Hunt was hardly there for two months before she passed. It may not even need new paint. Oh, yeah, and 125, or maybe it's 127. I think the guys wrapped up work on that last week. I'm not for sure on that, because that was the day my baby got sick, and I had to leave early to get him from day care?"

Interactions with Rhonda took a bit more time.

For one thing, she was hard to track down. I'd hear her voice and follow it like a trail. She was a social butterfly, moving through the facility singing, slapping backs, and shaking hands, her hearty laugh booming off the walls as she balanced paperwork and a plate of food.

"Ms. Erin," she would start, and I would tell myself to

slow down and be polite. Rhonda took offense if you didn't meet her gregariousness with equal measure.

"Now how are you today?" she'd say. "You are looking quite sassy in that dress, yes lookin' good, my friend, lookin' fine."

"Well, thank you, Rhonda." I smiled. "And do I detect a new perfume on you today? You smell delicious, like fresh vanilla and roses."

Rhonda grinned and shook her head with laughter. "Don't I wish that old man of mine might buy me something fancy like perfume." She laughed again. "Nah, I think this is just my Suave bodywash you're smellin', Ms. Erin."

After our initial pleasantries, Rhonda was all business. She'd put on her glasses and look at the list with its rows highlighted in pink, green, and yellow.

"You do NOT, I repeat NOT, under any circumstances want to show 125," she said. "That room is all jacked up. You hear me? Jacked up. I don't even want to talk about it right now." She shook her head with disgust.

"I am thinking you show 210. Mr. Weech moved out a few months back, and they just slapped down the carpet last week because, remember, his plumbing was messed up. That took six weeks to fix up."

I undoubtedly did not remember this, but Rhonda was a fount of information regarding everyone and anyone who stepped into Stratford. She made it her business to know the details of your life as intimately as you would allow. Whether it was the fact that you lost your right big toenail last week because you dropped a box of books on it, your cat was found asleep in the clothes dryer (happily alive), or you had a cousin who owned a tractor dealership in Pipestone, South Dakota, Rhonda would remember. Her mind was like Wikipedia, with daily rewrites.

By the conclusion of the headquarters meeting about Darla, I had developed a composite picture of her. She was a woman of an indeterminate age, and her curly hair had a tinge of gray. She was very particular about food, one of her few pleasures, along with her love for painting. Darla was so obese that she required special equipment be ordered for her apartment. Frank knew what type of vehicle Darla would need to transport her from Charles Dickey's Place, as well as the brand of bed, easy chair, and oversize toilet that would need to be brought to her apartment. There had been some additional discussion over the width of her apartment door and whether it would accommodate her girth and her personal mobility device (PMD).

Frank had noted that Darla was perfectly capable of walking but preferred her PMD. She was known to be a reckless driver, and some of the managers suspected she had even manipulated a physical therapist into tinkering with the PMD's mechanics because it could achieve unusual speed. When Darla was incensed about something, she would barrel down the hall, admonishing whoever had not given her what she wanted.

When I returned to Stratford, I asked Rhonda if she knew Darla.

"Yes, ma'am, we all know Darla," she said.

For the first time since I met her, Rhonda seemed non-plussed. We were standing near the front desk, and though I had used my "indoor-HIPAA-compliant" hushed voice, Jewell, whose hearing was phenomenal, leaned over the desk in our direction.

Jewell was just about the most bodacious woman I had ever seen. She routinely donned sexy tops and sweaters, and sported designer jeans with flashy embroidered back pock-ets. Her makeup was always portrait-studio ready, with fake eyelashes, shimmering lavender eye shadow, and a manicure with tiny gems on her long nails. Her voice wrapped you up like a hug, sweet and demure.

"Darla, you say?" Jewell's eyelashes fluttered. "Now that woman is gonna be some trouble."

Rhonda and I sidled up to the desk.

"Why do you say that?" I asked, sure some invisible line had been crossed by even tendering the question. Rhonda and Jewell exchanged a knowing glance.

"She used to live here a long time ago. She didn't get along with the other residents. Always bickering, always complain-ing. Nothing was ever good enough for her." Jewell stopped, figuring she probably said enough.

Rhonda looked at me as if she hoped the good Lord had time in his day to save me. Inwardly I sighed. Little did I know that dealing with Darla would become one of my greatest challenges at Stratford.

My concerns were borne out when she moved in. Darla's

wants were as deep and wide as the Atlantic Ocean. The suffering she had endured in her life had turned her into a petulant, feisty, morose, manipulative, and dreadfully unhappy person.

Darla was one of the loneliest people I had ever known. Her intelligence, combined with her scathing anger over the abuses she had suffered in her life, led her to punish anyone she didn't trust. And she trusted no one. She would sound alarms that had half the building scurrying to assist her, only to discover some minimal issue—her remote control needed fresh batteries, she was out of toilet paper, she wanted her trash emptied, and so forth. Days would go by with no demands from Darla, and the staff and I would tiptoe past her in the hall, shoulders hunched in anticipation. And then it was as if something inside her, loneliness perhaps, would erupt. Her hand would press the call button in her room relentlessly. When staff hurried to her door, asking what was wrong, what did she need, they'd find her in her lounge chair, her purple legs swollen with edema on her ottoman, her flesh naked, and tears splashing furiously down her face. It seemed she wanted the caregivers to find her that way, as if she wanted to expose her internal pain, daring those who attended to her to turn away.

Sometimes she and I would meet with the two ombudsmen in the conference room. Like a queen on her throne, Darla would enter in her PMD, stiff and aloof, wielding the power apparatus like a scepter. I would listen as she described all the things that we had done wrong in the building, the suffering she had endured, and who had caused it. I took notes, wrote down names. I asked questions. When she became too furious to continue, the ombudsmen would answer for her. I told her I would investigate and take action to address her concerns. Sometimes she thanked me perfunctorily and left. Other times she would sense that I was challenging her—not the veracity of her complaint, but whether what she wanted done about it was realistic. I could not just fire someone because she demanded I do so. I could not just move another resident out, have only one nurse or one caregiver take care of her. I could not assign one person to care for her twenty-four hours a day.

Eventually Darla and I would develop an entente of sorts. Our mutual stubbornness had come to an impasse. She would continue to make unreasonable demands and throw periodic tantrums, while I would continue to paste a gentle smile on my face, summon a sense of calm, and explain to her what I could do, and what I could not, to appease her. There was not a soul in the world, let alone a single caregiver or other staff member at Stratford, who could make Darla happy.

19

CAREGIVERS

This story would not be complete without the caregivers.

These were the women and men whose jobs included wiping creamed corn from the bony chin of an elderly, toothless man. Who cleaned up after residents who had ejected fecal matter on the walls and floors of their bathroom because of failing digestive systems, and who would rub diaper cream on sore parts after. These caregivers spooned pudding into shrunken mouths that popped open like baby birds' beaks. They washed hair—red hair, black hair, white hair, sparse hair—massaged oil into braided and combed locks, and pinned up tresses prettily with clips and bows.

They wheeled, propped, lifted, tucked, massaged, and turned one body after the other to avoid bed sores; they worked socks over stiff feet and pulled compression hose from legs thick with edema. They helped modest people maintain their dignity, shielding them as they helped put on loose pants and tops, soft shawls, and plaid woolen jackets.

Those who did not care about modesty, they gently coerced into clothing that would cover what had been exposed.

For the caregivers, there were countless boxes of rubber gloves, in sizes small to extra large, in the nurse's stockroom. We were always running out. If someone came down with E. coli or the flu, the entire staff used them for an instant wipe-down. Then we would run out of Handi Wipes, and someone would have to run to Walmart to pick up more, since supplies usually wouldn't be delivered for another few days.

Residents who were sick were quarantined, but it often wasn't long before several more came down with the same illness. Contagion surged like wildfire through the building, and at those times the caregivers' fatigue was replaced with a look of anxiety. No one ever knew how long it might take before the last case was diagnosed and the last person returned to health. The threat of illness cast a somber atmosphere over the halls.

The caregivers were on their feet, in Reeboks and hard-soled clogs, most of their eight-hour shift. They moved around so much it was rare to see a caregiver wearing a sweater, despite the fact that the thermostat in the common areas registered a cool 68 degrees.

Sometimes in an attempt to assist a resident, a caregiver would forget the rules and take on more than they could handle. They would lift a woman twice their size from where she fell on the floor instead of waiting for the nurse and the power-lifting machine. The next day, when the pain in their back was so bad they couldn't climb out of bed, they would confess what they had done, and I would file a worker's compensation claim on their behalf and report what happened to whoever required the report. The staff member would be out for weeks, if they came back at all.

Caregiving in an assisted living facility extends beyond the fundamentals of attending to health and daily needs. At any given time a caregiver could be a chef heating food in a microwave or stirring cream into coffee, a referee attempting to break up a disagreement, a surrogate family member, reminding the resident how important they are and coaxing them to perform the burdensome daily rituals that keep them in this world.

Caregivers are part-time house cleaners, furniture movers, notetakers, interpreters, rule enforcers, and armchair therapists. They are all that and so much more. The work of caregiving is difficult, relentless, and full of sorrow. They should all be given medals for their first month of work and for every month they stay beyond that.

On the whole, the caregivers at Stratford were wholly competent, but their lives were nearly as awash in quandaries and loose ends as those of the residents. The good ones—the ones who were both purposeful in their caring and adept at managing difficult personalities—came and went like rain in the Portland forecast. The troublesome ones, with a bag of caregiving tricks, were there to stay. So long as they showed up to work. On time. For the whole shift. As long as they weren't hiding in the closet to take extended breaks or discovered accepting trinkets and chocolates in a resident's room, with their feet up on an ottoman as if they owned the place. If those caregivers left, it was always abruptly.

Why did they go? They didn't like being told what to do (whether by a resident or their supervisor). They were packing up the kids and moving to Reno (leaving the surly boyfriend to come home to an empty apartment). They'd heard about a waitressing job through their cousin. (Sure it was the late shift, but at least all they had to do was swat old men's hands off their tush, nothing they hadn't had to do as a caregiver.)

These caregivers were often the residents' favorites. After they disappeared, an angry posse would show up at the front desk, asking for me and wanting to register their complaint.

"Why did you get rid of Carmen?" they demanded.

"I didn't get rid of Carmen," I answered. "Carmen left of her own accord." This was never a satisfactory response to those who had now lost someone else they loved, someone who looked them in their eyes and listened as their hearts spilled over.

The stable caregivers came in several varieties. For some, their whole life had been taken up with caring for others, aging parents with heart disease and varicose veins, a drug addict sister in and out of rehab, or a cousin's unmanageable children. These caregivers lived on cold toast, black coffee, and three or four hours of sleep a day. They often worked two jobs and were the first to sign up for extra shifts. They could hustle up any number of people to pick up the kids after school or take their grandma to her rheumatologist if they were running late. Their scrubs belied the challenging nature of their work, patterned with pink and blue cartoon bears or a cluster of rainbows. Their garb declared that they were kind and patient: *You are who I care about; you come first.*

Among the caregivers there were also saints, employees who had found their calling in life. It seemed there was nothing they would not do in the course of taking care of the residents. Their smiles, their humanity, their focus, and their touch were so genuine that on more than one occasion I found myself searching for wings on their back. Nothing fazed them. They showed up early so they could spend time greeting residents and asking about their evenings. They volunteered to help whenever an extra hand was needed (and somehow were always nearby when it was). They hummed quietly or sang out loud as they went about their work, hugged and clapped joyously, and encouraged and complimented all who crossed their path. They were paid between ten and twelve dollars per hour. Time and a half if they worked more than forty hours in a seven-day period.

These caregivers didn't mind disorder. All the noise, the piles of stuff, the childish behavior, the tantrums, the puking, the refusing to eat something, the anger at authority, the endless complaints, and the countless times they heard, "You don't understand me"—the caregivers just took it in stride. Stratford and every other ElderHome facility would have to shutter its doors without the likes of the caregiving saints.

20

BODIES, BABIES, AND
A BROKEN MARRIAGE

The health of the residents at Stratford made me very aware of my own well-being and all my body had gone through over the years. Like many girls, at around age ten or eleven, I had started to notice physical differences between me and my friends. Superficial things like the thickness of a ponytail and the left or right curl of fingers and toes, as well as more crucial developments like the shape of emerging breasts. Those of us who were unsure of ourselves began to long for what we did not have. A flat rear end. Attractive green eyes.

Dissatisfied with what I was born with (thick calves, a substantial behind, and an underbite), I focused on how my body might be tested. I endured "daily doubles" practice before and after school in soccer, as well as late nights on the basketball court. On weekends I would push my body to run three to five miles and then do a hundred sit-ups behind the closed door of my bedroom. Some other girl was always better at these things than I was. Some teammates appeared to fly across the field with the soccer ball stuck to their foot like Velcro. They'd launch themselves at the basketball hoop and propel the ball soundlessly through the net. Their faces remained serene and focused, with barely a sheen of sweat on their brow. Every physical activity I engaged in felt exhausting, as though bricks were bound to my limbs and oxygen was failing to make its way into my lungs. And then there was my unrelenting hunger. I wanted to eat everything; nothing satiated me. And after I ate everything in sight, I was always full of regret and self-loathing. It was a painful, never-ending cycle I could not seem to break free from.

As I entered adolescence, I was afraid of boys, so I dressed in ways to not attract attention. I was neither large nor small, "a perfect medium size," noted my friend Roxanne, who had developed early and had a tiny waist and large boobs. Boys blushed nearly purple whenever she sat next to them in class. My chest was still flat, but I had an embarrassingly peach-shaped rear end, instead of the no-hips and flat-butt boy shape I coveted. Roxanne wore size zero Gucci jeans that I would hardly have gotten one leg into. I settled for shrink-to-fit Levi's and my father's old button-down shirts, which covered me to my thighs.

As the years passed, I mostly got over these feelings of inadequacy. I came to appreciate certain aspects of my figure and worked hard at forgiving its imperfections. I still relied too much on what others told me they liked about my body. I had read enough feminist texts that I should have rejected the notion of caring about these things at all. Yet, I *did* care immensely and stupidly. I was familiar with the abuse women inflicted on their own bodies. The bulimia, the cutting, the starvation, and the excessive exercise. I dallied with some of this myself. It only made me feel worse.

After I turned twenty-one, things got easier. I just gave up on hoping for my body to be something other than what it was. I started to run a lot more and took pride in how far I could go, took pleasure in the rush of endorphins.

As a young wife, when I decided I wanted to be a mother, I didn't spend much time mulling it over. I got pregnant with Camille easily, within six weeks of my going off the pill. I didn't have time to consider how pregnancy would permeate my body and my mood.

During the first trimester my hair sprung into curls and darkened, and I was in a constant state of nausea. I consumed boxes of saltines and craved anything citrus. I continued to run a few times a week, wondering if the baby felt the jostling. My doctor assured me she was suspended as if in a sturdy balloon, protected from any danger.

I faced pregnancy as seriously as I took on any major project in my life, assiduously adhering to the recommendations in the insanely popular book *What to Expect When You're Expecting*. My doctor was a rotund man with a soft voice and bushy salt-and-pepper beard. He was laconic, but his friendly eyes sparkled at me when he entered the examination room, like a young Santa.

"Drink wine," he suggested, noting the anxiety that

surfaced in our conversations while he ran his warm hands across my burgeoning belly.

"But the book says . . ." I gazed up at the ceiling, as one does while surrendering to monthly checks during pregnancy.

"Women in France drink wine their entire pregnancies," he noted. "Their babies all turn out fine. It is more important you relax. One to two glasses a week won't harm you or the baby."

I considered this but only took him up on the suggestion twice, on New Year's Eve and on my birthday in April, close to my delivery date. The wine didn't really taste that good, nor do I recall it providing me with any sense of ease.

I am not the first woman to suggest that pregnancy and giving birth is not easy. Our bodies house our developing child for nine months of our lives, while we endure stretch marks, puking, massive veiny breasts, and swollen ankles. And then we push out our baby with herculean effort, all the while putting up with spouses, nurses, and doctors who are meant to ease us through the event.

I was in labor with Camille for forty hours. Scott and I drove to the hospital and were sent back home twice before the staff agreed to admit me. I was still only dilated to one centimeter, so things must have been a little slow that night at St. Vincent's. I pictured the nurses giggling back at their station, whispering things like, "Poor mama has a long way to go." Camille's birth felt like a marathon.

Scott and I went through rounds of uncertainty at each step, feeling completely ignorant despite labor classes in preparation, a pile of books on pregnancy and childbirth, and consultations with midwives. I would crawl off the hospital bed in agony and immediately heave myself back on. I would ask for water and only be given ice chips. In quieter moments I would try to regulate my breathing.

I seemed to have lived several lifetimes by the time the doctor told me Camille's heart rate was slowing and that possibly the umbilical cord was wound around her neck. If I didn't dilate to 10 centimeters soon, "we" would have to do a C-section. With newfound fortitude, I demanded an epidural. I was not going to have someone cut me open, not a chance! Finally, a couple of hours later, Camille's huge head tore through me, and the doctor silently unwound the cord from her neck as her narrow shoulders and bluish body came into view. I gasped at the sight of her scrawny legs and misshapen skull. She cried meekly, and then, as if prompted by the doctor holding her by her two feet, with more gusto. I instantly forgot everything that had happened over the previous two days. I held her against my naked body and cried. I was in love.

The few hours after birth are when your love for your child is as enormous as all the undiscovered galaxies in the universe. You would give birth to them again and again and again. But the honeymoon of those first few weeks can be short lived. I had never been so sleep deprived in all my life. As a couple, Scott and I adjusted to parenting poorly. We fought over diapers, breastfeeding, and whether Camille should share our bed. Scott would often storm out of the house in frustration, and I would breathe a huge sigh of relief, as though a winter storm had just passed through. These scenes are how family dynamics are formed, with unresolved issues and exchanges that play like a scratched record over and over throughout a marriage.

Along with the hints of marital problems, my autoimmune disorders—Hashimoto's thyroid disease and scleroderma—took root during this time, though I didn't realize it. My Hashimoto's, once discovered, was addressed with synthetic thyroid. It took years to get just the right dosage, and my hormones fluctuated wildly in my thirties, causing a roller-coaster ride of tremendous highs and mind-blowing lows.

The scleroderma was another story. There is no cure and no set timeline. Patients may live ten years or until they are eighty. I received the diagnosis dumbly, as if the doctor had handed me a train schedule and pointed to the station, but I had no idea of the destination. I have had the disorder for more than twenty years now, and I follow advice on how to manage the symptoms to be "more comfortable." For the Raynaud's that causes extremely cold hands and feet due to poor circulation, that means finding ways to stay warm. For carpal tunnel syndrome, I'm supposed to avoid gardening, tennis, cooking, typing, and yoga (all of which I partake in to some degree), and wear hand braces at night. For the stiffening cells of my face, hands, lungs, and heart, I undergo annual echocardiograms, pulmonary breathing tests, and longer appointments at the dentist. And, of course, every doctor's order includes the admonition to eat a healthy diet, get plenty of exercise, and avoid stress.

I couldn't escape the stress that was increasingly obvious in my marriage, but I nevertheless wanted to have more babies, many babies. A year or so after Camille was born, I got pregnant and had a miscarriage. For a week or so afterward, Scott treated me uncharacteristically delicately. Soon, though, he returned to arguing with me over everything having to do with child-rearing, our respective work priorities, and why I didn't enjoy our neighbors stopping by the house whenever they felt like it, asking for a little "help" from Scott on fixing a leaky sink or hole in their roof, which took him away for hours. We found ourselves in a constant state of friction. Having Camille had only seemed to exacerbate whatever unresolved childhood fears and disappointments drove him to now-routine fits of anger. I was tired of trying to ward off these fits, and increasingly protective of someone else, my daughter.

One long night during a vacation on Martha's Vineyard, I left him and Camille in our quaint inn at 2 a.m. and walked for miles in sleepless agony, thinking of all the different paths I could take. Envisioning the life my daughter would have with Scott's escalating anger toward me, while I patiently stood by, was like facing a storm brewing out at sea. When the storm hit, which I felt was inevitable, we'd be shivering on the shore, salt and sand burning our eyes, our clothes in tatters, our home washed to bits. But what scared me more at that time was what would happen if I left Scott.

We ended up staying together then, and I swiftly got pregnant again. Gunnar's birth was easier, and this time

I was able to watch the sequence of events with a mirror placed at the end of my bed. It was a different hospital from the one where Camille was born. The lights were soft and low, I was given extra blankets to stay warm, and the event felt less businesslike.

Gunnar's narrow body slid out of me like a seal emerging from the sea. He was the cleanest baby I had ever seen, with a fluff of long eyelashes and perfect arching feet. As the nurse handed him to me, his umbilical cord still attached, his naked limbs clawed the air, and he rested his sweet face on the exact spot on my chest where my heart was beating. Scott stood next to us, tears on his cheeks. I could see in his eyes the hope for us to have a new beginning.

The sense of partnership that stemmed from having created our perfect little family with a girl and a boy was fleeting. Two children were much more work than one and required us to stay more aligned, to face in the same direction with our parenting. If anything, we started to take completely different paths, both digging in our heels, both seeing what we wanted for our children, and for ourselves, through a unique lens. Separation was inevitable this time.

Camille and Gunnar were four and two when I left Scott. I found a mint green house to buy only a mile away from the house Scott had renovated for our family. Our divorce was ugly, fraught with histrionics and mutual despair.

It took two years of shouting over the phone, a mountain of lawyers' fees, and a bitter custody battle to get to the finish line.

My attorney, Catherine, later told me, "Your divorce will go down in the annals of Portland history as one of the most contentious and certainly most memorable." She beamed at me as if I had won some sort of award elementary schoolers get.

I smiled grimly back. "I must get bonus points for the fact I was compared to Madame Bovary by Scott's attorney?" I said.

"Not just compared, Erin. He spent at least forty-five minutes providing CliffsNotes on the book and suggesting you had read it [which I had in college] and decided to live your life exactly as Madame Bovary did! I thought the judge was going to have a seizure."

In fact, it seemed to me the judge was half-asleep for most of our three-day trial, while I was bewildered and lost. My fate and my children's fate were in the hands of this man in a black cloak. The judge would make a decision that could change the course of my life. The thought of losing custody of my children was so horrifying I couldn't allow myself to think it, but it remained like a shadow in a dark alleyway.

The divorce proceedings were such a nightmare I could barely live through the months it took for the judge to write his final decision and share it with us in the courtroom. Afterward he rose from his podium and left through a side door, as I gazed after him, contemplating what lay ahead.

Finally, the mail brought the final decree: the dissolution of our marriage and a notice of my primary custody of our children. The brief history of Scott's and my lives together was ended with seven pages of paper. There was no place secure enough to hold that documentation of my freedom. I purchased a grey metal file box and placed the decree carefully inside, along with Camille's and Gunnar's birth certificates, a black-and-white photo of a beloved neighbor who had died when I was at college, and a record of my childhood immunizations saved by my mother.

An era was over. It was time to look ahead.

21

DAILY RITUALS AND
SPECIAL OCCASIONS

On relatively quiet days, if you didn't peer too closely, Stratford had the appearance of a slightly run-down apartment building in the inner city. It was low-income housing, yes, but with extras that let the residents feel as if it was not their only choice. To me it was always a bit of a mirage, a stage set for everyday life.

Many of the residents had only known tumultuous existences up until then. I was not privy to everyone's details, but I knew of registered sex offenders, former thieves and drug dealers, prostitutes, and people who had lived on the streets. Intermingled with them were simply unfortunate souls who had lost their money to greedy children, been unable to work due to a work injury, or who had been devastated by disease and medical bills. There were those whose hearts had been broken, the mentally ill, the beaten down, and the frail and weak.

Nevertheless, they all expected to live a normal sort of life with daily routines of coffee and the newspaper and weekend visits from family and friends. Everyone had their own key to their studio or one bedroom. They could come and go as they pleased. Meals were available in the dining room during set hours, and an ice machine churned out ice all day long. But there was so much more, because the residents needed so much more.

What the facility provided was a framework of support, because if these people could have made it on their own, they would not have come to Stratford. When they arrived, they were frequently malnourished and in need of medicine or a bath. They came with grocery bags full of their few worldly possessions. Sometimes they were accompanied by a family member. Other times they were led in by a social worker looking for a placement. When I met with someone new, their emotions ranged from humility or indifference to agitation. They did not always want to be there, nor did they always belong. One person might be like a feral cat, itching to get back outside. Another was full of bravado, boasting of how they did not need anyone. Someone else was unable to look me in the eye, couldn't answer my few questions, couldn't remember the last place they lived.

Our census ranged between eighty-five and ninety-five while I was at Stratford, and it was at mealtimes that we saw most of the residents together. There were ten tables in the dining room; each could sit eight. Some residents never left their rooms to eat. We had limited tray service for those who were under the weather or agoraphobic; their meals would be delivered to their room. We had a handful of people on hospice or just counting their days. These people barely ate at all.

The dining room scene reminded me of a college cafeteria. Some folks sat in the same chair with the same neighbors at the same time every day. Others were ostracized and had a hard time finding a seat where no one shouted at them to go away. Some residents were thick as thieves. Others hardly spoke to their tablemates, and I wondered if they even knew each other's names. It was companionship in silence.

The food served was of great concern to me. Here, just like at college, our residents tended to gain a "freshman fifteen" pounds within weeks of moving in. Breakfast was scrambled eggs, sausages, home fries, and the occasional fruit cup. Albert, the head cook, added southern spice and fat to virtually every menu item. His specialty was pork spareribs dripping with smoky sweet barbecue sauce, accompanied by collard greens stewed in bacon and butter, and cornbread smothered with more butter and honey. Ice cream was dished up on request at lunch and dinner. Salad came as precut iceberg, shredded cabbage, and carrots from a plastic bag. Steamed vegetables were swimming in melted butter. Salt laced everything like a dusting of snow on a cold wintry night. The coffee was lukewarm and lackluster. There was nothing organic, nothing fresh.

Although we had a dietician who was assigned to our building, she was at the mercy of the USDA food program requirements, which bewildered me. Here were people being fed the food prescribed by the federal government as nutritious who were clearly gaining weight and developing health issues or worsening the ones they already had.

I couldn't even eat the food Albert made. I tried, sitting down a couple of times to socialize with the residents over lunch. I merely picked at my food and watched as many others did the same. To me, despite my adolescent battle with eating disorders, food has always meant love. Food should be wholesome. It provides fuel and lets us unwind and ease into the segments of our day. At Stratford, food struck me as dangerous.

The dining room was also the site of special occasions, like the celebrations of life that tended to occur with little notice. We might have an inkling a resident was near death, but their actual demise, of course, could not be predicted. Although I might have hoped for some advance planning, most often Rhonda would simply announce that Mr. Maxwell's remembrance was to be held in the dining room at three o'clock, just after snack time and an hour before Ms. Maeve's ninety-second birthday party. Mr. Porter would be playing the piano; Mr. Maxwell's nephew, who was a preacher, would be saying a few words; and she, Rhonda, would sing.

Ensuring that everyone arrived on time to these events was another matter. Residents and guests rolled in both early (to get a good seat and first crack at the snacks) and late (on their own schedule). Earnest folks—those who knew the deceased, were related to him or her, or just enjoyed a spectacle—sat in chairs lined up near the piano and the mic. Others hovered by the door. When the preacher spoke, he moved back and forth in front of the group like a stand-up comedian, and the crowd rewarded him with the occasional "Praise Jesus!" and "Amen, that's right!" If the sermon seemed to be off subject to me, with little mention of who had died, no one else seemed to mind.

When Rhonda took the mic, all commotion would quiet down. Everyone was familiar with the golden sounds that came pouring forth. She had no formal training, but she had grown up singing in church, and she loved being center stage. Some residents got up and danced while Rhonda sang. Others clapped to the rhythm and shook their head side to side. Rhonda beamed, as she threw her head back in jubilation.

Usually very few family members chose to speak. Death itself in an assisted living facility often comes after months of anticipation; most families are worn down by the time it arrives. They have said their goodbyes. They may even be worrying about which relative might be next. Auntie Rosa has been forgetting where her keys are, and cousin Tyler has been laid up with complications from his diabetes. Grandpa Harvell was found miles from home on a park bench. Someone is always calling the doctor for so-and-so, driving them to the store, filling a prescription, and sitting quietly by their bed as they rest. The winding down of life evokes memories of the past and concerns for the future, both retrieving and releasing them.

Sometimes I would stand with others by the door of the dining room, knowing I might have to leave abruptly for a meeting. Other times I would sit among the residents, taking in the spectacle like that small girl at the ballet. The residents would ignore me and, generally, each other. Perhaps death felt too close for them to enjoy sharing the moment with anyone else.

Birthdays were quite different occasions. Not everyone received equal attention, though. One day Sam, who was blind in one eye, leaned on his cane by the front desk and reminded Jewell it was his birthday.

"Is that right, Sam?" She winked at me. "I thought last week was your birthday. Or wasn't it in November?"

Sam looked pained. His mouth drooped.

"No, it's not November, Jewell. I told you that before. It's today!" Jewell nodded and raised one finger as she answered the phone. Sam was now near tears.

"What plans do you have for your birthday, Sam?" I asked. He glanced up at me with his good eye and just as fast looked away.

"Nothing much," he muttered, not moving. "Maybe have some friends over, maybe some cake. Raspberry cake. That's what Mama used to make. Buttercream frosting. Raspberry cake." Before I could answer, he walked away, indignant, his head held high.

Other residents were treated like royalty, their birthdays the highlight of the week. Miss Lonnie was one such queen, in part because no one was entirely sure of her age, somewhere between 99 and 110. Miss Lonnie had no recollection of where or when she was born, just that it was springtime and coincided with the birth of twin foals from her favorite horse, a rare event. Family stories said that Lonnie's mother had been forced to catch her own placenta when the midwife ran from the room after hearing the roar of surprise from the men in the barn.

Lonnie was completely deaf at this point, and her legs swung uselessly from her wheelchair, her pink slippers hovering over the floor. Just seventy pounds, she could be easily lifted from one spot to another by anyone who cared for her.

Everyone was drawn to Lonnie's sweet smile. She loved to have her hair styled. Some days she had braids with pink ribbons tied to the ends. Other days her fine white hair would be pinned back with a pink rose tucked into her bun. Pink was her favorite color, and, on her birthday (which staff had decided was April 3), the dining room was awash in pink cupcakes, pink streamers, pink balloons, and pink punch. Lonnie was made up with spots of pink blush on her cheeks and wore a pink sweater with pearl buttons over her pink housecoat. It seemed the entire building had turned out. It was standing room only. And in the center of the room sat Lonnie, regal and serene, nodding and patting each person who came to hug her and kiss her hands.

For the healthier, more active people in the building, birthdays were an opportunity to "tie one on with my girls" or head out to the casino in Grand Ronde. Stratford's activity director organized a bus outing there at least once a quarter. It was a popular day trip that had a waiting list of residents eager to put their money in the slots and sit at the craps table with a club soda or whiskey. They sported new hairdos and fancy wrist bangles, sport jackets, and shined loafers.

Children and pets were a rare sight in the facility, though therapy dogs were beginning to make an appearance. Officially ElderHome did not allow pets in the building, but if a case was made, and the care team approved, small pets could join their owners. These residents had to be mobile and able to take their pet outside to "do their business," or capable of emptying a litter box or hamster tray.

In my view, most of the pets seemed forlorn, despite their owner's constant companionship. A dog might rest by the side of a resident's chair; a cat might curl around a resident's neck. A hamster's cage might come to rest so near the base-board heater that running on the wheel would leave the little rodent panting near its water pipe. While the resident required the warmth and adoration that the pet provided, the animals always looked doleful to me.

Grandchildren, nieces, and nephews visited on occasion. After five minutes of questions about their elders ("Why does Grandma have those tubes up her nose?" "Why is Grandpa so fat?" "Why does it smell like potty in here?" "Where is the soda pop?"), their interest would wane, and they'd slip out to explore the building with its many curiosities and people to spy on. They'd dart through the halls, toppling plants and garbage receptacles. Residents would move out of the way as fast as they could, holding the wall to steady themselves, their eyes lighting up in fear and delight at the giggling whirlwinds whistling by.

Whenever possible, the activities director would steer the kids to a sitting room where puzzles, drawing implements, and board games might entertain them. (There was a TV, too, though it sometimes mysteriously disappeared, only to be found in one of the residential apartments.) If no one corralled them, though, the kids would enjoy the run of the building until Pam came bursting out of whatever room she was working in and chase them all with her broom, her cheeks rosy with laughter while the children squealed with delight. Pam, despite her wild eyes and energy, was a natural mother, and children gravitated to her like bees to honey.

22

THE MEANING OF FAMILY

After the divorce, I led the life of a single mom for roughly eight years. I had my job, I tried to take care of my health, and I dated a little. But Camille, Gunnar, and I would eat together every night, no matter how late the hour due to after-school activities. We needed this nightly ritual, sharing giggles and tears as we rolled out the events of our day. I was the anchor at the end of the six-person table. Camille sat to my right and Gunnar to my left. I often had a martini, shiny with the promise of my forgetting, just a little, how difficult it was to be a working mother and single parent.

Camille ate voraciously, having never met nourishment she didn't delight in. Even as an infant she had ravaged my nipples with endless, angry sucking, as if hoping for something better.

Gunnar, however, had been a picky eater as a child, even throwing up after every meal; it had been such a common occurrence we hardly flinched when he bent over his empty plate and painlessly regurgitated what little he had just consumed. The texture of certain foods seemed to bother him. White fish was too slippery and flaky, yogurt too runny, and eggs were just strange looking. He preferred broccoli, carrots, chicken fingers, and bread. He had a similar sensitivity to items of clothing. Polyester, for example, was too dry and unyielding for him. He wore only fine cotton blends, soft wools, and flannel. I imagined he'd grow up to be an aesthete or a monk. As it turned out he gravitated to veganism, recycled clothing, and atheism by the time he was twelve.

The medical explanation for Gunnar's routine barfing was called gastroesophageal reflux. He grew out of it sometime around age seven, and once that peculiarity stopped for good, his distended stomach and puny arms started to fatten up.

It was a while before I had a sense of Jay's kids' eating habits. Jay and I had been dating for close to a year before his ex-wife allowed me to meet Cole and Ava, who were eight and five then. The wait truly tested my patience. I am a calm and chill mother (Ava has told me), until I lose it over something relatively inane (according to Camille). I realized the late-night phone calls from Jay's ex asking him to wait longer before bringing their children into our sphere was a last-ditch effort at controlling him. The maneuvering got my hair in flames. I believe in just jumping in and getting things over with. The white-glove treatment my two future stepchildren were receiving over my introduction to them seemed ridiculous, especially since I had known their mother since college, before I had ever known Jay. Jay finally just stopped taking those calls and set a date for an introduction dinner.

We ate at Sandoval's, a decent Mexican restaurant down the street from my house. The kids eyed each other and squirmed in their seats, as kids do when they are trying to figure out the lay of the land. They questioned each other's food orders, refused to laugh at our usual jokes (instantly united in rolling their eyes at the adults), and howled uproariously when it was unwarranted.

Cole and Ava quickly noted that Camille had a cell phone, which she obtrusively texted away on until I told her to put it away. The boys tested out a bit of banter to see if they could make each other snicker. Ava and Camille completely ignored each other. It went well, as far as Jay and I could gather, and I was exhilarated that the silly blackout period had ended.

After Jay, Cole, and Ava moved in, mealtimes remained important. We sometimes ate as late as 9 p.m. so that the last child could be picked up from their sport or activity and we could all be together. At the first family dinner in our house, Ava plunked herself down in my spot at the end of the table, closest to the kitchen. Given my pragmatic approach to stepparenting—which meant that I tried to keep the peace publicly, even if a thousand annoyances itched at my insides—I sat down to the right of Camille. Jay presided at the other end of the table, and Cole took the remaining spot, to the left of Gunnar. This arrangement would remain exactly that way for years and years. Even if someone was out of town, at an overnight with a friend, at the other parent's house, or on a business trip, we adhered stolidly and inexplicably to our self-assigned spots at the dinner table.

The exception was when Jay and I had a rare night with no children at home. We would sit at the bar in the kitchen—we had named it the Jay Bar—with a martini by our plates. Jay became a mixologist after I convinced him he needed to take the gin bottle out of the freezer. He was not one to take a good tip and let it end there. He had to become the resident expert. He bought countless cocktail books, barware in brass and silver, coupe glasses, and bamboo picks, and we tried virtually every gin among the ever-expanding choices at our local liquor store. A nightly martini kept us moving forward at the end of every long day.

The landscape of our lives raising four strong-willed young children together was uneven and ridden with potholes, black ice, and slick mossy rocks. We had to find our way to rules, both spoken and unspoken, to guide us through.

Throughout these years, I clung to the belief that if each child had a room to call their own—to run to and slam the door or choose to invite others in—they might be more likely to get along. Each of them could be who they were. That was one of my primary tenets of raising children: Love the child for what they were born to be. I would help guide them toward their best selves, even if I had little control over how that manifested itself. I could certainly set household rules and require basic development of goodness, fairness, and hard work. But when all else failed, I could send them to their room, which would not be complicated by a sibling or stepsibling sharing that space, having an opinion, blasting music or videos, and generally stirring the pot.

To accomplish this, I sacrificed my need for a room of my own. As a teenager, I had read Virginia Woolf's essay on the subject but never had the privacy, income, and good food (well, maybe the latter) that were necessary for a woman to write. As a single mother, I worked long days to put that good food on the table, but my income moved in and out of my bank account every month with little left over as I covered the expenses of raising these individuals I was intent on letting go into the world. When the three of us became six, the quiet time I required to reflect, read, and put words on paper shifted from random moments to nonexistent.

Every room in our house was chock-full now, with a child, their things, and their loud, diverse, and emotional personalities. Questions and exhortations filled the air: "Whose T-shirt is this?" "Whose Lego set?" "Why must we have five thousand DVDs lined up by the television?" "Whoever had a soccer/basketball/tennis/golf game today, please pick up your crap!" And to add to the chaos, we adopted a five-year-old dog from the Humane Society. Teeka became the glue that bonded all of us together, allowing us to tease her and laugh at her silly dog behaviors when all we really wanted to do was yell at each other.

I did find time to keep up my running, which was a source of solace for me. A few nights a week I left work by 4:30 p.m. to take Gunnar to his soccer club practices. These were generally held on fields in the heart of Beaverton, and traffic was thick during rush hour, so I would bring my running gear and jog in wider and wider loops around the neighborhood.

As I ran, fantasies unwound like a film reel. In my mind I was perpetually skinny, bright-eyed, and refreshed from a good night's sleep. I was a published writer, with strong enough sales to allow me to own a house by the sea where I would go to on weekends to write.

In my head, Jay's and my children all earned good grades in high school and ventured off to noted institutions of higher learning, while Jay and I reveled in our empty nest. We'd learn to make wine, take ballroom dance classes, and travel to exotic places like the Canary Islands and Madagascar.

The time would fly as my wonderful imaginary life streamed through my mind. When I arrived back at the field to catch the final minutes of Gunnar's practice, the endorphins flowing through my veins would throw a blanket of calm over my body. I would feel the pure joy of being a mother, loving my child as if my heart might break, watching him being himself.

I had to give up on the idea that my stepchildren would be anything at all like my biological children, just as I had to give up on the idea that my biological children would be anything like each other. Every one of them had a unique quality: Gunnar's ability to convey his love through his written words. Ava's infectious laugh and whimsical view of the world as her oyster. Cole's serious formality in so many things and his unabashed adoration of his father. Camille's powerful roar, despite her small stature, which both frightened and embraced us.

Jay and I encouraged their individuality and their diversity of thoughts and opinions. Mealtimes were the scene of debates and long silences, as well as insults, apologies, tears, and laughter. We evolved from eating tuna casseroles, hamburgers, and enchiladas toward healthier ingredients, working our way through alternative grains (quinoa, farro, barley), a variety of milks (almond, hemp, coconut, rice), and exotic vegetables (turnip, leeks, eggplant, fennel, kohlrabi, chayote). The children ate it all. When the dinner call came, they emerged from their respective rooms like gophers. They lined up to serve themselves from the bar and sat in their respective seats under the glow of the candles we always lit.

Jay and I would tell them how lucky they were to each have their own cell phone (which were not allowed at the dinner table). Their eyes would grow wide as we described taking the *one* rotary phone in our respective households (which incidentally had *one* bathroom) down the hall to our bedroom (in my case shared with a sibling!), wedging the cord under the closed door so we could talk privately to our besties. Or how later, when we actually had two extensions, we had to scream at our siblings to hang up, when we knew they had picked up the receiver in another room to listen. We would tell our kids these stories so they would know just how good they had it.

Like many families, we celebrated holidays, birthdays, rites of passage, and achievements with much fanfare. We established our own traditions, such as picking out the Christmas tree and decorating it together on a Sunday

afternoon in early December, spending an hour or so with
fireworks out in the cul-de-sac on the Fourth of July, and
building poster boards of childhood photos for each kid as
they graduated from high school, when we threw a big bar-
beque in our backyard and invited all the friends and family
who had watched them grow up. Along the way, each child
let us know in their own way if something was working or
not. We adjusted and metered our focus more heavily on one
over the other, depending on who was struggling the most at
the time.

It was a lot of work, as was balancing our new reduced
budgets and sorting out our respective new jobs. At times it
seemed we were barely hanging on; our mental and physical
fatigue was real. Other times we were thrilled to find ourselves outside on the patio on a summer afternoon, a cold
drink in hand, watching the tomato plants grow. Our home
life, our children, and our marriage were what saved me from
a complete mental breakdown while I worked at Stratford.

To be sure, some nights I would wish all the kids would
just stop talking. I would long to return to the time Jay and
I went to Puerto Vallarta and found ourselves on the beach
in the Zona Romantica. There after our morning yoga class
and lunch at Joe Jack's Fish Shack, as we lolled on the sand
with our paperbacks, sunscreen, and beach towels, a cheerful
waiter walked our way through the soft sand, as if he had been
waiting to see us all week. "Cervezas mis amigos?" he asked.

But I had chosen all this. I loved Jay in a manner I had
not believed was possible. When I woke up in the morning,

I never questioned anything but the truth that we would be together for a very long time. Forever had always seemed like such a trite word to me. It was enough that I knew the two of us were permanent, like one of the 150-foot fir trees that bordered our property. Its branches periodically needed trimming, but its body was rooted in the ground.

23

PARIS, BARCELONA, AND THE GALAPAGOS

Jay and I had decided against a honeymoon. When we got married, we were still reeling from our respective year of mutual unemployment, and pulling off a wedding, even one with barely sixty guests, had been a stretch for us financially. On the other hand, Gunnar's Twelve-Year Trip with me loomed on the horizon. We had been planning it for at least eighteen months; our deposit was paid, our passports were newly minted, and weekly missives had started to arrive from the National Geographic tour company that would guide us through the Galapagos Islands.

The premise of the Twelve-Year Trip had come to me when I was newly single and dating Alex. He was the first to catch my eye on Match.com, an enticing and intellectual man almost thirteen years my senior. In our first few months of dating, Alex and I spent late evenings over strong drinks at romantic bars all over Portland, seated just close enough to trade opinions without getting too turned on (though we usually ended up at Alex's dilapidated turn-of-the-century house). Our topics of passionate discourse ran the gamut from religious cults, Marxism, and Libertarianism to what people were doing in Dubai, medical tourism, and sex. (Alex had been raised in a cult and had only recently discovered all that was available in the pantry of sexual pleasure. He was like a kid at a candy store with barrels of different sweets, wanting to sample each one.)

During one of our intense exchanges, when Alex was in the midst of detailing how his father had raised him to "be a man," I interrupted him with the excitement of someone who had just had a brainstorm.

"You know," I said, "I was thinking how all religions seem to have a rite of passage, which is the turning point for a boy to become a man or a girl to become a woman. I am talking about something spiritual, ceremonial." I went on. "A transfer, where the child crosses an invisible or visible line. Where the adults provide them with the opportunity to experience the world in a different way. And young persons suddenly see themselves not just as 'self' but as part of some greater group, that of womanhood or manhood itself."

I could tell I had piqued his interest.

"Aha," he said. "So, you are thinking of Cami and Gunny on this front, no?"

I nodded.

"You know I am agnostic," I said. "And so, for me, my vision of a rite of passage for my children would be to expose them to something uncomfortable, to take them out of their element and allow them to acknowledge their own personal strengths, their fears, their passions. I want to show them the path, not lead them down it.

"There is Rumspringa in the Amish community, which translates as 'running around.' This is a time in an Amish teenager's life where their parents encourage them to explore the company of their peers. They participate in more organized social activities, are encouraged to court each other, sometimes even use unsanctioned technologies or learn to drive a car. Rumspringa ends ultimately with baptism in the Amish church and marriage. Technically this is a choice made after seeing or experiencing a bit of the world outside the community, and few choose to leave it.

"There's the American Indian vision quest," I continued, "the solitary vigil to find one's spirit guardian, which is really just another way of saying the search for one's identity and personal strength. And, of course, we are all familiar with the Jewish bar and bat mitzvah. In this case, the idea is that one cannot truly participate in public worship without a sound grounding in the religious precepts of Judaism. There is education and practice, and one is put on display. One must demonstrate knowledge that is shared among the larger adult group. How different that is from a young boy going off into the woods alone on a vision quest; his right to return is based on his own self-recognition and reliance.

"I neither want to throw my children deep into the forest with wolves nor submit them to a crowd of chanting elders. I want to observe the change that occurs within them, either because I was there when they experienced the change or because I witnessed the evolution of their selves afterward. You still with me?"

Alex nodded indulgently.

"So, here's my idea. Granted, this is a highly personalized and first-world choice for a rite of passage. I want to offer to take my children wherever they want to go in the world when they are twelve. Just the two of us. They can choose where and how they want to go about it, within reason, of course. Let's just say, it must be something I can afford, but I won't put too many fences around it. They can conceptualize where they want to go and how they want to experience it."

"I like it," Alex demurred. "I can already see that they will each choose quite differently. And will you accompany them the whole trip, like a chaperone?"

I thought about this for a moment. "Yes. At twelve, I don't believe they are completely capable of insulating themselves from the danger that lurks in the world. I won't hover, and I'll put them in situations where they can explore with loose restraints. But I will be near. I will be their protector and their witness.

"In the end, I want them to discover how uncomfortable they can be waking up in a strange bed, in a strange country, with a peculiar-looking breakfast on their plate, street signs that are impossible to interpret, and vistas of unfamiliar and fascinating buildings and foliage. There is something that happens to your soul when you cross fear with wonder; it conjures up possibilities of one's future."

I eventually parted from Alex, but the idea of the Twelve-Year Trip stuck.

Camille had chosen Paris, followed by Barcelona. I stumbled a bit by inviting my mother to accompany us, which Camille would never let me forget. She felt she had lost out on something by not having my undivided attention during the journey. I had so successfully built up the allure of this rite of passage that as much as she adored her grandma, I suspect Camille thought her transformation had been diluted.

My mother had moved to Portland shortly after my divorce, after living in Bisbee, Arizona, for several years. Before that she spent a year licking her wounds in Tasmania. Her marriage to Maurey had ended when he found his way back to the bottle and shared it with his former wife.

Along the way my mother had changed her name from Sandra to Tif'eret, which meant "path to enlightenment," according to her interpretation. She had come to Portland, armed with her ability to reinvent oneself, and she helped me do so as a newly single mother with a big job involving frequent travel. She would stay with Camille and Gunnar often, one of the many ways she helped me survive that challenging era. However, she had developed a poor back and weak leg from bad hips after she turned sixty, so Camille's adolescent energy was also stymied a bit on our trip abroad.

The overnight train between Paris and Barcelona was fraught with discomfort and stuffiness that led to a lack of sleep for all three of us. But both cities were magical in their own way, and Camille and I managed the occasional escapade without her grandma, who was content to stay back with a cup of tea and her journal. We roamed the Champs Elysées, marveled at Notre Dame, and explored the Parc Güell and Barri Gòtic. We drank sangria together, and she shopped for clothes like a child movie star. By the time we came home, she had already set her sights on future European travel, college in Chicago or New York, Prada handbags, and Chanel perfume. I saw the woman she would become, a fashionista, food critic, and music lover, adoring daughter, and friend to hundreds who loved her confidence and panache.

Ever the nonconformist, Gunnar chose his destination by spinning the plastic globe in his bedroom. His left pinky landed near the islands off Ecuador.

"The Galapagos!" Jay exclaimed, always fervently supporting Gunnar's fascination with unusual places and their even more unusual cuisine. Gunnar had discovered Anthony Bourdain around age nine, and he and Jay watched nearly every single episode of all those travel food shows together.

Gunnar raised an eyebrow and asked what was interesting about the Galapagos. Having studied Darwin in high school and the history of South America in college, I was delighted by the idea. Something about that part of the world sat well with my poetic side, as well as my love of the sea, and I thought it would be fascinating to see flora and fauna that existed only there. I described for Gunnar all the wonders of the Galapagos: the blue-footed boobies, the volcanic rock islands, the turtles and iguanas, and the surrounding sea. Gunnar was transfixed, and we put together a slideshow for him to present to his fifth-grade class, once it dawned on us we had inadvertently booked the trip to leave just before his fifth-grade graduation and the last day of school.

Gunnar always seemed to be on his own schedule, a day early or a day late through no fault of his own. It's part of what has made Gunnar who he is—unconventional, awkward, and simultaneously appearing both older and younger than his years. He had a big, active brain and an innate kindness toward and acceptance of others that seems to fit more with humans of the future, people who finally understand what it means to say we are all the Other.

Gunnar's experiences in the Galapagos were more in line with my imagined initiation into adulthood. He faced several challenges on the trip that tested his personal strength and fortitude, like a classic hero on his journey. Odysseus trying to find his way back home from the Trojan War, Alice in Wonderland, Gulliver on his travels. On our first night in Guayaquil, Ecuador, before heading for the islands, he found himself locked in the hotel stairwell, caught between the first floor where he could not exit and the rooftop where he could. He ran up and down in a panic for what seemed an eternity, until a security guard discovered him and returned him to our room.

On the boat, he mingled with the twenty other children traveling with their parents, navigating impatiently among the families' various rules of oversight. With his natural jocularity and crooked smile, he made friends with all the adults, too.

During the daily outings to each island, however, Gunnar was truly in his element. He ran the trails with endless energy, staying at the elbow of the tour guides, absorbing their knowledge about every species, every rock, and every plant.

At the Charles Darwin Research Station, we both stood by the low-slung fence that enclosed the home of Lonesome George, a Pinta Island tortoise (*Chelonoidis abingdoni*) and the last of his kin. In his final years, George was considered the rarest creature in the world. Born in 1910, the tortoise died in 2012, a couple of years after Gunnar and I saw him. The researchers had attempted to breed him with female tortoises that were a related species, but nothing came of it.

As Gunnar observed George, I talked out loud to the animal, as I had with my children when they were babies. Innocuous chatter, asking about his day, his breakfast, whether he was sleepy, and so on. Gunnar put his arm around my waist and leaned into me protectively, as he had done since he was old enough to walk. It was a gesture that never failed to unsettle me. As his mother I was supposed to be doing the protecting. But Gunnar's empathy for all species instinctively led him to comfort others.

By the time we got to Quito for the last few days of our trip, I saw self-confidence lighting up Gunnar's face. He wanted to get a five-dollar haircut; he wanted to see this park and that museum. He was leading the way, even as I lamented that this beautiful adventure together was coming to an end. I longed to stay, to watch animals in their natural habitat, to eat fish so fresh you could taste the sun and salt, to be rocked to sleep in our little cabin on the boat again, gazing through the portal at the moon over the dark blue sea.

When I returned to Stratford after the Galapagos trip, I was stunned by the contrasts: In place of an open sea where I swam with the sea turtles and enjoyed the feeling of salt drying on my skin in the sun, there were suffocating walls, angry residents, and overwrought caretakers. For nine days I had experienced bliss and cherished the memories I shared with my twelve-year-old son. Now I was back to bleakness, fighting off tears daily, avoiding my abusive boss, and never getting anything right. The jarring differences were illuminated like a landscape lit up by a lightning storm.

24

THE INVESTIGATION

I had experienced depressions in my life—during my unhappy adolescence, throughout my early years in college, and after Scott and I had separated—but the depression I descended into working at Stratford was truly suffocating. Daily life was a struggle. It was difficult to get out of bed, turn on the coffeepot, and brush my hair.

I felt as if I were at the bottom of a dry well, begging for a glimpse of blue sky. I couldn't breathe, except during yoga or in my sleep. But even then, my sleep was disordered with frightful dreams, about giving birth to dead babies, about past loves falling out of a broken window in an empty Victorian house, about snakes hissing at me from inside the garbage disposal or flicking their tongues at my face.

I was listless during the workday, but I masked my fatigue with a false enthusiasm. I had always been a believer in "putting on a brave face," as my mother taught me. When I got home, though, I would collapse. I would still make dinner, do laundry, find some way to get some exercise, but I went about these tasks and activities like a zombie.

Sometimes I would break down and cry in front of others, usually with my mother over the phone or on walks after work with two close girlfriends. When I painted the picture of the insanity that was Stratford, they would cluck-cluck supportively, shake their heads in indignation, and hoot with amazement. At those moments, the depression peeled away, like sunburn flaking off my back.

All of this was so painful its memory is still deep within me almost a decade later.

I had been at Stratford for just over a year when the first accusatory letter arrived at the ElderHome headquarters, and I was called into the business offices of the health system by the newly appointed director of ElderHome. Eva had replaced the womanizing drunk who had held the position for years, and I was nervous about the meeting, though I didn't exactly know why.

My manager, Icky Vicky, was also in attendance, sitting in the other chair with the look of a self-satisfied cat on her face. Her expression made me want to slap her or at least reach down the back of her neck and expose the price tag still attached to her brand-new sweater. Her unruly hair was especially badly done that day, pinned back up in a make-shift bun the size of a walnut.

I had never trusted Vicky after the first two weeks I knew her. Weak, unaccomplished, and disliked by everyone, she was pathological in her pursuit of self-aggrandizement, shining a light on herself at every opportunity. She carried on a relentless campaign of removing anyone she thought might be in her way or who possessed the actual qualities she lacked. I was convinced she lied, stole, and obfuscated at every turn but had insufficient evidence to back that up. Mostly I just wanted to be rid of her. Her presence as my new manager was bringing my need to leave Stratford into keen focus.

Eva had barely hung a family photo in her new office, when Vicky convinced her that Wendy had too much on her plate. Within weeks, Eva had split Wendy's role in two, with Vicky at the helm of "housing" (which meant I reported to her) and Wendy maintaining "member services." The crossover of these two operations appeared to no longer matter. Vicky seemed to lick her lips and ponder her next move.

I suspected that I represented everything that Vicky despised; I was stubborn, self-possessed, and not from the neighborhood. Vicky evidently considered me obstructive to her own upward mobility, and she wanted me out of the way. Ironically, she had been on the panel that hired me, grinning in a welcoming way but hardly saying a word, letting the others ask the questions. She was like that, always sitting on the outside, never center stage. Then suddenly she would speak up, and it would be like a flash fire in the corner. Whatever she had to say was challenging. She'd point a finger, call someone out, and suggest something bad was afoot.

For her, the cause of a problem was always race related, and she brought it up in a way that made people squirm and left them wondering if in fact they had done or said something inadvertently offensive. You had to be very careful in anything you said to Vicky. She'd reframe and twist your words until they were not at all what you believed or intended.

"A letter has arrived," Eva said, after I had sat down in the windowless room.

"Oh?" I said.

"It claims that you do not like Black people in general." Eva coughed, uncomfortable. "And that you have made racist comments at Stratford to employees."

I sat upright. I was appalled. I refused to look at Vicky. "May I read the letter?" I asked.

Eva shook her head. "No, I am afraid I cannot let you do that. It's anonymous," she finished. As if that made any of it any better.

She went on to say that because there was only one letter, they would let the matter go for now. They didn't ask me how I felt or what I thought. They didn't give me any instructions or ask if any of it was true. It was not.

When we walked out, Vicky strode ahead of me, her purse tucked under her arm as if I might grab at it. She didn't speak and didn't look back.

The issue of race had arisen once before at Stratford, at the facility's grand opening, about a month after I had started working there. One of the more vocal leaders from the surrounding Black community appraised me gruffly and turned to Wendy. "No offense, mind you," he said, "but are you telling me you couldn't find a Black person suitable for this role? What kind of message do you think that sends this population, and this neighborhood?"

My initial reaction was shame. For what? For being white? For having the guts to do something I had never done before among people who might not want me there? Who were highly suspicious of me even though they didn't even know me? I was an outsider, and this man's question reminded me of that. I wondered deep down if the shame and discomfort I felt was about the clear path I had found myself on to being hired, despite the fact I was an outsider, despite the fact I was new to Healthcare administration, and had only just obtained my master's degree. At the same time it struck me as a reasonable question, for which I wish I, or Wendy, had a better answer.

On that occasion Wendy did her smiling best to give the gentleman a broad-brush summary of the recruiting process, which was meant to exclude no one and encouraged diverse candidates to apply. I am sure it sounded like a canned answer. The man listened politely, his eyes keenly focused on both of us. He then turned to the group gathering in the room, clapped his hands together and launched into a welcome speech, congratulating all on the new ownership by ElderHome and the associated improvements at the facility.

After the meeting with Eva, my depression turned into anger. Fuming, teeth-gritting anger. How dare I be accused of racism? I was rattled. I was hurt. Nothing in my upbringing, my schooling, my personal beliefs had prepared me for the accusation. It burned and mortified me. And it began to push me over the edge. I could feel a trickle of motivation to get out. I went about my duties at Stratford methodically, while a mantra of hope took root in my mind. *Move on. Move on. Move on. You cannot fix any of it. You can do better. Move on.*

And then there was a second letter. Once again I was called into the windowless room, but Vicky was not there this time. Instead a Human Resources representative looked at me grimly and advised me that this time there would be an investigation.

I asked how long I would need to stay away from work. She said maybe a week or so. It depended on how long it took to meet with every employee in the building. I left, feeling as if I had just stepped out of the Tilt-A-Whirl at the state fair.

I should have been relieved for the paid break, but my head felt as if it had been cracked open with a meat cleaver and left all my pain exposed. The weeks since the first letter had been uneventful, but now I couldn't think straight. I was suddenly paranoid, fearful of what might be hiding around the corner. Someone wanted me out. I wanted out, too, but not like this.

I turned to a friend of mine who was an attorney. I remembered what had happened to a woman I knew who had been unjustly accused of trying to unionize fellow employees at the health system where I worked. She had only worked there a year and had made a few smart-ass remarks to friends. All she had wanted to do was complain over the watercooler to some co-workers. Someone, however, had tattled on her, and those remarks grew out of proportion until it sounded as though she was trying to organize others into action.

She was cornered by Human Resources, ostracized by

her peers, and told to not come to work while an investigation took place. She fought back hard, and after lawyers got involved, the company let her go with a year's severance.

She told me her story as we watched our daughters play soccer, her hands stuffed in her puffy coat, her tone icy and stiff. It was taking her a long time to find work. One night I ran into her at the grocery store. She had two bottles of wine tucked under her arm, two frozen pizzas, and a pint of ice cream.

"This is all I do these days," she said.

That image stayed with me as I worried about the investigation. My attorney friend told me to wait and see what the outcome would be. I wasn't even sure I wanted to fight. I could not imagine any good outcome. In my nightmares I saw Vicky writing the letters by candlelight, a Cheshire cat smile broadening her face.

The investigation took one week. During that time, I went to yoga every day, sent emails to former associates, and perused job openings online. I thought about my old office at Textron, the glass windows on three sides, the bucolic view of an old barn and a nearby stand with apples, berries, pumpkins, and flowers for sale.

I tried to forget the 2 a.m. call the previous week when Jewell could not get Charlie Hart's "girlfriend," Lila, to leave. Stratford did not allow unapproved overnight guests; they had to be on the list, and I was the one who approved them.

I arrived at the facility at 2:25 a.m. to witness Charlie yelling that he paid for it, he paid for it, damn it, and that we couldn't make her go. Lila was still standing there, wearing tight leather black pants and a fake fur coat. She saw me come in, untangled Charlie from her arm, and ran from the building as best as she could in her tall open-toed mules. I couldn't help noticing her toenails as she passed. They were perfectly polished in scarlet with a yellow rose on each of her big toes. Not a nick on the glossy polish.

"I got paid. I paid for her," Charlie kept repeating. It was the day when the checks from Medicaid arrived, and residents who were suspicious of direct deposits would line up at the front desk so that Jewell could hand them their cash. The white envelopes disappeared into their belts, their hats, or sometimes into the hands of greedy friends and family who just happened to stop by for a visit with Auntie or Grandpa on the same day money arrived from the state.

I looked at Charlie, whose eyes were darting from the door to me to Jewell in an unsettling spin until finally he loped off to bed, grumbling.

At the end of the investigation week, late on Friday afternoon, I got the call from Eva advising me I could return to work. Her usual awkward speech was curt.

"Nothing was found," she said, sounding mildly disappointed. I pictured her in her gloomy office. "Everyone seems to think highly of you, the staff anyway. They all said you were great to work with. No mention of racist remarks or an uncomfortable environment under your leadership." Her words fell off me like soft-tipped darts.

I didn't say anything. What could I say? I told you so?

My pride had never been so tested. I waited for anything remotely close to an apology. Nothing.

A schoolgirl giggle bubbled up and almost choked me. I was stronger than all of them, I realized. I had control of my life; I would get the fuck out of there if it killed me, on my terms!

"Thank you, Eva. I will see you next week."

Move on. Move on. Move on. You cannot fix any of it. You can do better. Move on.

25

THE ICE MELTING

Maybe it was the investigation, maybe it was being yelled at by a resident one too many times, maybe it was the constant calling out of staff, the drain of supplies, or the never-ending turnover of residents, but sometime toward the end of my first year at Stratford, I realized I was flat-out done. I peered at my wardrobe in the morning and chose one of three pair of pants that still fit me, a baggy sweater, and comfortable clog-like shoes. I had long ago abandoned the work attire from my prior life. I shopped for sweaters and slacks and ugly shoes that looked as if they could survive a mudslide, tornado, or worse. And I had put on weight, thanks to sodium-rich, fat-imbued snacks from the kitchen.

I passed a brush over my hair and rubbed lotion under my dry red eyes. I felt as brittle and uninteresting as a day-old baguette. If it weren't for the distraction of finding creative ways to feed, clothe, entertain, and educate our four offspring, I might have stopped making the effort months before. I drove to Stratford almost robotically, my mind closed off on anything but what was straight ahead: getting through another day so that I could climb back into my car and drive home again.

There was never a good reason why I stayed for as long as I did. There were a host of reasons. Fear of losing my house and the money for the kids' extracurricular activities. Pride and unwillingness to admit I made a bad decision. A need to prove I could make the facility into a success, a place where all things ran perfectly and no one ever got hurt.

I sensed that my family, primarily my mother, Jay, and Camille, had no idea why I hung on so long. I wore my stubbornness like a mantle.

It took several specific events to finally push me to the wall.

There was the time Jerry Fleming coldcocked Stewart Spinney outside the dining room with a nightstick. "*Where did he get that thing?*" the caregivers yelled at no one in particular as the facility erupted in a near riot at the scene. Stewart lay flat on his back, crumpled like a marionette, with one leg askew. I feared for the worst, but the med aide assured me he still had a hearty pulse.

Jerry stood nearby, almost patiently, the nightstick dropped behind him as if he could cleanly separate himself from it. There was a chorus of clucking old women and nattering old men shoving each other to get a better view. Jewell strode over and with a few admonishments scattered them like pigeons in a square. No one ever knew what the fight was about or if there even was a reason. According to the stories, Stewart had taken the last slice of roast beef from the buffet, when

everyone knew Jerry's favorite dinner was roast beef and potatoes. Or Jerry had a grudge from high school when Stewart
had asked a girl Jerry admired to the prom. Or Stewart and
Jerry were attempting to settle an old gambling debt.

Or Jerry just wanted to hear the thwack of a nightstick
hitting another man's skull.

What else pushed me over the edge? There was the night
Veronica, a caregiver nearly six feet tall with huge hands, the
most brazenly beautiful face and Rubenesque curves, came
storming into my office announcing she had found a loaded
gun in the middle of the hall on the third floor. She had picked
it up with a newspaper she grabbed from the activities room
and, with the delicacy of a diamond seller displaying pre-
cious stones on velvet, laid it gently on the table in my office.
I shied away from it as if it were breathing. I was speechless.
Veronica crossed her hands over her chest and looked at me
as if I was responsible.

"It's crazy to think someone just *dropped it* on the dang
floor," she said. Yes, I thought, yes, it's crazy to think that.

Shortly after that, another caregiver, Tina, as petite as
Veronica was tall, entered a resident's room to find the
occupant had vanished, leaving only the residue and accou-
trements of a heroin habit. A metallic smell permeated the
empty studio like the ash blanketing Portland after Mount
St. Helen's eruption. Tina tiptoed to the window and
opened it wide, brushing to one side the grime on the sill as
she glanced down at the courtyard below. No one ever saw
the resident again.

Above all, there was the repeated mental abuse from Vicky who made frequent surprise visits to me in an attempt to find out what I was doing (because apparently she had nothing better to do herself). If it was something wrong, she could admonish me publicly or privately. If it was something right, she would take credit, always publicly. Up until that point I thought I had a good understanding of wrong versus right, but Vicky had made it her primary goal to prove to the whole facility that I was incompetent in my job and generally an imposter.

The terror I felt in her presence would start to gel hours before I knew I might have to face her. I was like an abused wife, watching the clock over the stove as I peeled carrots for my husband's dinner. *What kind of mood would he be in when he got home today? Will he be on time? If he's late, that means either he stopped at the bar or his manager made him work after hours. If he's on time will he notice any dust I forgot to wipe from the coffee table? Will he think I over-salted the meat?*

I had never felt such utter hatred and raw fear of someone in my life. Not even my erratic ex-husband engendered the kind of loathing this woman evoked in me. With her as my manager, I was no longer the strong-willed woman I had been my whole career, organizing people, completing daily tasks and projects with pride.

I was not the same person who had walked into the unfinished space of Stratford for her interview. That sunny woman, with a just-earned MPA in healthcare, had been ready to jump in, get her hands dirty, and unearth a new passion for working in long-term care. Where was she now?

I looked at my children every morning as they trucked off to school and prayed they would never have to feel this way.

At Christmas the supervisors who reported to me, Director of Nursing Myrna, clinic nurse Sarah, head social worker Lydia, Chaplain Mike, and Dr. Swidwell all pitched in for a gift certificate for me at a local yoga studio and health center. I nearly swooned at the gesture; tears pricked at my eyes like pine needles. Why hadn't I thought of this? A way to take care of myself, a few hours of meditation every week—wasn't that just what I needed?

I was embarrassed that they all could see my anxiety and stress so clearly. I had always taken pride in my ability to maintain a calm demeanor. But I had learned by then that one of the markers of those who work in the health-care profession is that everyone *sees* you. They see your scars, your pallor, your broken fingernails, your weary eyes, your manner of walking, of speaking, of responding. They are used to peering at you closely and really listening, then cross-checking what you are saying with the medical history on your chart. In the business world, in contrast, people choose to see only what they want to see, often based on power and position.

Healthcare workers, however, must protect themselves from the despair, the loneliness, pain, and discomfort they witness. They need an emotional barrier, a suit of armor. The armor allows them to leave a seriously ill man after a short conversation about his vitals and go out after work with a friend for drinks and snacks. It allows them to deal with blood and excrement in the bed and on the walls, to hold a woman's arms until she stops clawing at her face, to approach desolate family members about a terminal diagnosis, and somehow move on with their day.

This was the armor I never put on. Instead I absorbed everything. The pain of the lives of the residents at Stratford infiltrated me like cancer. I had no barrier, no filter, and no boundaries.

When I went home Christmas Eve, carrying a basket of gifts from many on my staff, it dawned on me that they cared what happened to me. I had been coming to work every day like a zombie, so caught up in my determination to make it through another day that I never noticed their concern. I was self-absorbed. Exhibiting a positive attitude was like wearing a too-tight corset; I couldn't breathe.

When I pulled up in front of our house, small blinking jewels of light dappled the front lawn, reflecting the glimmer of the multicolored bulbs on the Christmas tree in the front window. I sat in my car and allowed myself a smile as I thought about the four kids sneaking a shake of a present under the tree, counting how many were addressed to each. Inside was the puzzle table in the corner where Jay was bent over the pieces, a cold Manhattan by his side. In the kitchen would be the fresh crab Jay had plucked diligently from the shell, a variety of artisanal cheeses arrayed on a plate with water crackers and Greek olives. Even after our income dropped in half, we allowed ourselves the indulgence of aristocrats now and then. Especially on Christmas Eve.

The kids shared our delicacies. We were not the type of parents who fed their kids macaroni and chicken nuggets first and sent them off to bed. Our date nights provided for time away from them. Though then all we did was talk about Camille and Gunnar and Ava and Cole. We talked about them as if they were songs we were writing or works of art. These children would be our masterpieces: our *Starry Night*, our *Children Playing at the Seashore*.

Tomorrow was Christmas, and at Stratford some of the residents would be sitting by the lights of the tinseled tree in the front room, the empty stockings hanging over the gas fireplace, two men playing a game of checkers in the corner. That image was like a painting I would put out in the garage with other things I no longer needed, things I wanted to forget. A painting consigned for a rummage sale or left by the curb with a handwritten sign—*free*.

26

UNRAVELLING

It was March, and Jewell was going to Hawaii with her boyfriend, who worked in the kitchen as a server. In her absence Mimi, a roving front-desk manager who primarily worked at a sister facility, was filling in. Mimi had a heart-shaped face and a short brown bob with a fringe of bangs. Unlike Jewell (or me for that matter), Mimi had the patience of a horse hauling a covered wagon full of home-steaders through the snow. Nothing seemed to faze her, and the residents were in awe of her. While they would complain frequently about Jewell or Jeannine not doing this or that or ignoring them (a complaint they voiced about everyone at Stratford), they addressed Mimi tentatively and politely, with the kind of deference reserved for a dignitary. She did not put on airs; she just seemed approachable. And once approached, she had an answer for everything.

Mimi was in command yet friendly at the same time. I looked forward to her occasional appearances. She confided in me once that Stratford was her favorite place to be.

"It's so full of energy," she told me. "There is always

something going on, and there are such characters here." She smiled genuinely. I admired her positive spin on things, so unlike my own dire view of Stratford. It seemed that Mimi had never been sad, confused, or lost, as if she had grown up with lots of parental hugs and sunshine beaming through her bedroom window. She was inordinately capable. She could avert disaster and bring order to chaos like stirring cream into coffee.

I appreciated her more than anyone else at the facility, and she was one of the few people I trusted in all of ElderHome. One morning I realized that she liked me right back. It was a rare moment when we were able to talk for more than five minutes without interruption. A busload of residents had left earlier that morning for a casino trip.

"My brother died on this day," Mimi told me. Her eyes were moist even as her sweet smile remained.

"Oh, Mimi," I said. "I am so sorry. How did he die?"

"Drunk driver," she said. "Not him, the other person. The driver's side door ended up pinning him to his seat. We think he didn't suffer."

I told her again how sorry I was. I could tell the way her words came out slow and precise that the two of them had been close.

"It was three years ago, and I still think about him almost every day." Mimi looked out into the lobby, as if her brother would emerge through the doors.

"Do you know, the things I think about are when we were kids. I hardly remember him as a man. I just think of how he held my bike for me when I was learning to pedal. How we would pull pranks on our parents on Christmas morning, emptying our stockings behind the couch and telling them Santa never came." She smiled at the memory. "He liked black licorice and ginger beer. He ate Spam straight from the can. He would hold my hand in the tent at night when my family went camping because I was so afraid of owls and bears. He promised me he would always take care of me."

I thought about my own brother then, how he could make everyone laugh the way he told a story, even if it was the most unremarkable tale. How he hated onions and was allergic to shellfish. The way in which he looked up to me and loved me, despite my anxiety, my need for cleanliness, and my requirements that the world be an orderly and predictable place.

The next day I brought a small flowering plant for Mimi, a cyclamen with vivid magenta flowers. She hugged me silently and placed it on the high counter where the residents could admire it.

Whenever Mimi was covering the front desk, previously buried problems would surface. She found half-eaten bags of chips and candied worms and tossed them in the trash. She would attempt to organize papers that had been stacked in ungainly piles. She returned phone calls and passed messages to the residents, but between us we discovered mail that had never been delivered, funds missing from the safe, and grievances written by residents that had been hidden under a box of sweaters and ties. I understood that these discoveries were all evidence of Jewell's poor performance.

As in any business, there was a process for addressing employee concerns, and I followed it as I wrote up a performance plan. When Jewell returned from her vacation, we met one-on-one in my office. She listened as I talked, neither confirming nor denying any actions or inactions on her part, and she signed the written plan when I asked her to. Then we went on with our day.

A few weeks later I had a meeting with Vicky in my office. As usual I felt as if the air had been sucked from the room the minute she walked in with her phony smile. She asked me how things had gone in my performance conversation with Jewell. Had she signed the performance plan? When I nodded, Vicky asked if she could see it. I went to the file cabinet that contained personnel files. It was supposed to be locked, but since I had always worked in an environment where locking drawers was not necessary or required, I had left it unlocked. I pulled open the drawer and found Jewell's file, but after several minutes of thumbing through the folder, I turned to Vicky, who was looking at me with an expression I could only describe as triumphant. Sweat formed on the back of my knees, and I had a violent desire to grab her by her pink-cashmere-sweatered shoulders and shake her.

"It's not there," I finally admitted. "It was there yesterday; someone must have taken it." I realized just how lame this sounded. My heart was beating like a hummingbird's.

"Are you sure you had the conversation with her?" Vicky asked.

"Of course, I am sure, just ask Jewell!" I stammered, a little too loudly. Vicky glanced at the closed door, as if Jewell were on the other side.

"I already did ask her." Vicky smirked. "She says you never met with her. She didn't even know what I was talking about."

In that instant I saw how it was. The letters accusing me of racism and intolerance did not work, so this was another approach at eliminating me. It didn't matter that I had dug in my heels and done everything asked of me. In fact, I had succeeded very well in the financial aspects of my job. In the last few months, thanks to my steely resolve, the facility had gone from losing more than a million dollars a year to a positive net income of more than ten thousand a month. I had managed the completion of the remodel, the opening of the medical clinic, the hiring and firing of staff, and the celebrations inside and outside with the community. But I was not wanted. I was an outsider, and Vicky (among who knows how many others) would do anything to get me to voluntarily go. And if that failed, they'd find a way to fire me.

I sat back down and watched Vicky in amazement as she put another performance plan on the table between us, a performance plan *for me*. I could barely process the words coming out of her mouth. It was as though she were spitting tiny red spiders. I shook my head slowly, in answer to my own unspoken query: *Do I fight this?* I took a pen and signed the document with a flourish. As she was leaving, I spoke to her back.

"Make sure you don't misplace that, Vicky. Oh, and I would like a copy, too." She turned and glared at me.

"I will send you a copy," she said, and she was gone. I locked my office door.

That day I gave up. I didn't know how exactly, but I was going to find another position, and I was going to escape this nightmare job that I had willingly taken on fifteen months before. The Great Recession was abating, albeit slowly, and I did not know whether I would be able to find a job in finance again. That didn't matter. I didn't care if I ended up a barista, a bartender, or a house cleaner (which I had done to earn side money during college). I wanted to wake up in the morning without a sense of dread. I wanted not to feel as if I had been released from a trap, springing for freedom when I left work at night. I wanted to be among co-workers and customers who appreciated and understood me. I wanted it all to make sense again, to get a paycheck, go home to my family, and feel joy.

27

REACHING OUT

I may have been mentally ready to leave Stratford, but it weighed on me that there was still work to be done there. We were no longer losing money at the facility, and we had crossed over the break-even point three months in a row, but the improvements came at the expense of cuts that affected staff, supplies, activities, even the heating bill. Our census was still clinging to a number well below expectations, and turnover was high. I interviewed countless potential residents, but most were a poor fit because of healthcare or other needs that could not be managed by our reduced staff. Others would have had an undesirable impact on the existing population. During our first encounter they exhibited such surly, mean, or disturbing behavior that I knew if we had admitted them to Stratford, it would have been like dropping a lighter on a pile of dry sticks. I was frequently reminded by higher-ups that it was "my building." It was important that I assess each applicant keenly, because although I had the final say on who moved in, it was much more difficult to kick someone out.

So nothing was really getting better. It was, in fact, far worse. Eliminating staff meant fewer residents' needs were met. It meant less oversight of misbehaving residents. It meant staff was worn out, made mistakes, or failed to show for their shift. Cutting back on supplies had a similar deleterious effect. Residents sometimes waited half a day for a delivery of incontinence products, and there were delays in getting medicine to residents who were on strict medication schedules.

The reductions led to more and more unrest. I could sense disaster brewing. By the end of February, we were in lockdown. There is no other way to describe it. After much arguing among management, it was decided that locks would be put on all entrances into the facility. Residents and staff would require their own key cards to enter and exit. There would be rules about who else could come in and, presumably, who could go out.

The afternoon the lockdown decision was made, I sat in my office looking out the window at the residents who liked to be outside. It was strange to me that not once had they waved at me, banged on the window, blown me a kiss, or given me the finger. They acted as if they didn't even see me there, when I knew full well I was on display like a gorilla in the zoo. I liked to think that once they were outside, they could forget about everything inside for a while, and that included me, the person in charge, the person who was incapable of meeting their needs. I hoped that for them the world outside was still an inviting playground where they could get lost in their memories and ignore the leafless trees and gray days of February.

I turned to my computer and I started to write an email. I wrote to my confidants, the people who knew me best. I kept my story short, explained that the job wasn't working out, that I'd like to get back to financial services where I felt more at home. I asked for their help. I asked if they knew anyone or anything. Anyone looking to fill a position, anything coming up.

Many of those I wrote to were former colleagues from Textron. Despite time and changed circumstances, the feeling of family lingered, and we had stayed in touch through an intricate web of contacts. We never lost our love for each other, and when we gathered together we would resurface old work stories and make them gleam, stories about conferences we attended together in Vegas and salespeople who never closed a deal, about love affairs and swingers, holiday parties where people went missing early or stayed too long, and a myriad of other mysteries that still titillated us like ghost stories told over and over beside the campfires of our youth. There was so much that crossed between our personal and private lives at Textron that it became muddled for many of us, and we were mired in gossip and anticipation of what daring move someone might make next. We tolerated each other's foibles with an exasperated patience. Our work environment was a rich, moving, and, at times, embarrassing mix of people's deepest desires and most human bad choices.

After Textron shut down, there were people who landed at this company or that company and, once entrenched, found jobs there for other former Textroners. A solid group of thirty or so moved around like chess pieces to finance jobs in Lake Oswego, Tigard, and Portland, and I realized I could reach out to them. I mulled over their business email addresses, evidence of their gainful employment, and I lingered on their profiles on LinkedIn, which showed zero gaps in their history of working in the field I missed so much. All that gave me pause.

Though the economy was improving, the nightly news advised that this greatest of all recessions was not yet a recovery. I still feared being unable to pay our household bills, worried about getting the children clothing and basketball shoes, or enjoying the occasional night at the movies. What if I couldn't find something? What if it was worse than what I was currently experiencing? What if I fell even further down the career ladder?

Also bothering me was the fact that I had worked hard to obtain my master's in healthcare administration, and yet I couldn't see myself ever working directly in healthcare again. I wanted to run as far away as possible from it, like a woman fleeing a bad marriage with just one suitcase and a bus ticket out of town. I told myself that I shouldn't regret having obtained the degree, even if by most people's standards it "went to waste." I was a lifelong learner; learning itself had always been my greatest reward. However, I am also practical. It would be ideal if I could dabble in healthcare while I went back to finance.

I realized how much I had loved my former career. I enjoyed analysis, contracts, and doing deals. I was a businessperson, not a people person. I liked the distance between the seller and the buyer. I didn't want to touch strangers or be touched by them. Working at Stratford, I had discovered how sensitive I was to that kind of interaction.

Everyone I reached out to responded with emails full of encouraging words.

"How about coffee soon?" they wrote. "I am a little busy this week with an urgent project but would love to touch base and hear more about what you're looking for!" I latched on to the smallest positive response, the hope of a meeting that might lead to another that might lead to an actual interview for an actual job.

Then came the email from Sheila, a woman I had worked with at Textron and known at least fifteen years.

"Erin, I am so sorry things are not going well for you. You need to get out of there! Have you tried contacting John/Randy/Robert?" Her suggestions came at me like a freight train rushing down the track to a definite destination.

"No, should I?" I realized how shy I had become. My confidence in my past work experience was in tatters. *Get moving!* I admonished myself. Sheila's empathy and verve spurred me forward. She pulled me up from the depths where I was wallowing, like a strong hand extended to a drowning person. I grabbed it.

Not long after that I had a job offer at U.S. Bank, underwriting for healthcare customers. I had found a way out; I had found my way back home.

28

GIVING NOTICE

The day I gave notice was an ordinary day at Stratford. My nerves were raw, my palms sweating, as I prepared my resignation letter. I decided not to fold it into an envelope but instead slid it perfunctorily across the table to Vicky as she bustled into my office and pulled out her notebook, which undoubtedly contained a laundry list of items to bully me about. The letter stopped her briefly in her tracks, but she recovered almost instantly. Her creepy beatific smile masked some unknowable emotion—pleasure, disgust, or anger, perhaps—as she looked at me and let the letter drop on the table.

"You'll be leaving in two weeks?" she asked, as if willing me to admit I may have made a mistake.

"Yes, Vicky." I looked at her with what I hoped was the visage of a mother scolding a child.

"Okay." She fussily stuffed her things back into her bag, pulled her chair away from the table, and, with a glance over her shoulder, added, "Nothing really to chat about then. I have things to do to arrange for your replacement."

I nodded, but she was already gone, like a girl sneaking out of a disappointing date after the first course. I suspected the search for my replacement had started some time previous to that moment I told her I quit, but I had beat her to the punch.

Regardless, I wasn't nearly as satisfied as I had hoped to be. My fantasies of quitting in a wild rage, eyes blazing, papers flying around the room, in front of witnesses were far more exciting. Taking the high road, as I have learned to do my whole life, leads to disappointing results emotionally. I am always left with the feeling that the other person somehow got their way.

Everything that came after I resigned was just as draining as the moments leading up to it. There were all the questions from the residents, all the congratulations from my peers. There was Vicky's unending silence, as if I had let her down by cutting short her campaign to crush me. She need not have been so disappointed; little did I know the stress of working at Stratford would stay with me for years after. It horrifies me to consider how deeply that woman got to me. I still remember how much I wanted to return the violence I felt from her. My thoughts were very ugly during that time, very ugly indeed.

My final days at the facility were a blur of activity, and although I had stopped waking up full of dread, I didn't exactly feel as if I had won the lottery. If I was honest with myself, I felt disappointment. I had never admitted to myself that I was a failure at something, that I just couldn't cut it.

And in order to escape Stratford, I had taken the very first job I could find that would still pay my share of our bills. It was several rungs down the ladder from any position I had previously held in finance. I had been shattered by my time at Stratford, and I was humbled.

For the most part, the staff was supportive of my departure. Whether they agreed this was just not the place for me, or they never really liked me, or they felt sorry for me, or they envied my ability to escape from the pressure cooker that was Stratford didn't really matter. They did everything most co-workers do when someone has resigned. They gave me hugs and stopped me in the halls or at my office for short chats. They gave me more hugs. (This was a demonstrative place to work.) They brought cards and gifts and arranged a surprise breakfast. The last few weeks were the highlight of my sojourn at Stratford. I was blossoming with relief; my footsteps felt lighter, as did my brain. I suddenly remembered how to smile. I felt gratitude for the first time in eighteen months, since Wendy called to offer me the job.

It was June, and the sun shone every single day. I took extra breaks just to walk out into the courtyard and cast my eyes over the residents, the building, the parking lot, and the neighborhood beyond. I felt a curious need to commit it all to memory. I chuckled inwardly, asking myself why in God's name I would want to remember a single thing. I thought that if someone had zapped this last year and a half from my life, I could just go on as before. As it turned out, I could not. It took several years to come to a place where I felt recovered

in mind, body, and spirit. At that time, I had simply no idea
how much of an impact working at Stratford had had on me.

On my last day of work, I planned to leave after lunch.
We were having a residents' barbecue in the courtyard, fea-
turing a live band composed of several talented musicians
who lived at Stratford. There was Albert's famous chicken
and ribs, along with macaroni salad and rolls. I walked out
to join Myrna, Sarah, Lydia, Chaplain Mike, Dr. Swidwell,
and Rhonda, who were all socializing with the residents and
dancing in place to the music.

June, a talented artist and resident who mostly kept to
herself, approached me and put her hand on my arm. She
wore a gray beret and an oversize sweater over her denim
dress. Her brown orthopedic shoes were scuffed heavily on
the toes, as if she was in the habit of walking on them like a
ballerina. Her left hand was behind her back. I turned to her
and smiled. "Hi, June," I said.

"Hi, Mrs. Manager." She paused, suddenly shy. I waited,
and, emboldened, she moved her left hand forward and
shoved three thick papers into my hand.

"These are for you," she said. She had handed me three
watercolors. One was a pastoral scene of green, blue, and
yellow, with a brown cow bending to eat the grass. I flipped
to the next, a vase of flowers, all bright and cheery, save
for one red tulip that bent forlornly over the side. The final
one was of a blond woman standing by a desk, gripping
it hard with one hand and touching her forehead with the
other. A woman with brown shoes sat in a chair nearby,

apparently looking over the blond woman's head to the window outside. In the frame of the window only blue sky showed through.

I closed my eyes and could hear my heart beating. When I looked up to thank June, she was gone.

29

REENTRY

I walked away from Stratford as if on a rapidly moving conveyor belt. My old white Volvo station wagon flew home as if it, too, knew in its pistons and shock absorbers it never had to come back. I had imagined weeping with joy when I got home but instead felt like doing cartwheels on my front lawn. Everything around me was in Technicolor, pulsating with light.

Three days later I arrived at U.S. Bank Equipment Finance's offices, a two-story building from the 1990s, located in an indifferent office park, improbably parallel to the I-5 freeway. Small islands of desperate foliage sprouted up between rows of parking spots with room for hundreds of commuters' cars. It was not unlike other suburban parking lots I had pulled into during my career in finance.

I stayed in my car for a moment after cutting the engine, observing employees propelling themselves toward the doors of the building. In they piled, one after the other, their hair combed, their shoes shiny, a bright yellow handbag here, a smooth leather briefcase there. Some carried lunch coolers;

others sleepily sipped from large travel coffee mugs. Watching them, I felt as if I had returned from a long backpacking trip abroad, where I had traipsed through countries where I did not speak the language, could not decipher the restaurant menus, had lost the way to my accommodations, and had to use my hands and facial expressions to communicate.

Here I was, back in one piece, showered, fed, taking my first steps to rediscovering what it felt like to be comfortable at work again. To be home. I was not the same person, though. Not even one bit. I was determined to bring whatever good things I learned at Stratford (which I was working hard at documenting) into this more familiar past life that was now again my present. Over the weekend I had had time to reflect. I was not, in fact, returning to where I had left off in my finance career. I was hired at a more modest level, as a credit analyst. I would sit in a cubicle, one of more than 100 cubicles on one floor, surrounded by offices with windows looking over the parking lot and the freeway. I would have no one reporting to me. I would be an "individual contributor." I relished that last part; I needed to find who that individual was again so that I *could* be a contributor.

And no one would be asking anything from me emotionally or physically. I would only be asked to write, analyze, and report. I could handle that short list of demands. Because I knew I was capable of much more, and this work would require so little effort from me compared to Stratford, I could even afford to daydream, and no one would ever know.

I could feel all the sharp edges that had been holding me upright for the past year and a half begin to soften and blunt. I took a long, deep yogic breath and opened my car door. The hardest part of any new job for me is always the first few weeks, when I must meet people, smile generously, and behave like the extrovert that I am not. I viewed this as a sprint that I would force myself to power through. After that, I could fold back into my natural introversion and just do the work, go home, and never be called after hours because the front door alarm had gone off, or someone had a stroke in the dining room, or we had run out of hypodermic needles.

The woman at the front desk had large and fashionable glasses and short blond hair like a shiny bird's head. She reminded me of a female goldfinch. She smiled at me and offered me candy from a dish on the counter, while handing me a temporary badge. It was quiet as I passed a few moments looking at bland prints adorning the walls.

"Hello, Erin! You're here!" The boss who hired me, Steve, approached. His lopsided smile crinkled the skin around his eyes as he put out his hand to shake mine. I smiled back.

"Yes," I said, warmth springing up inside me as if his voice had turned on the tap water at a sink. "Yes, I am really happy to be here."

From there forward, it was like returning to work after maternity leave. My body had become squishy in places, my brain fragmented in others. I had been crying randomly from fatigue and a sense of hopelessness over the wants of so many human beings at Stratford that I had forgotten to take care of myself. My days had been like riding a Ferris wheel, round and round, while I wished desperately that I could get off the next time my carriage reached the ground.

One saving grace while I was at Stratford was the age of our children. As a group, they were on the cusp of adolescence or had not yet left childhood. But they were self-sufficient and self-absorbed enough to allow for my mental and physical absence and, sporadically, Jay's as well.

On the career front, Jay was nearly in lockstep with me. He had been forced to accept a lower-level contract position with no benefits for one of our local school districts. He left for work every morning, his shoes shined, a sparse lunch tucked into his briefcase. On the surface he was the epitome of a 1950s dad— proud, strong, no-nonsense, with dry humor—but underneath he was all kindness, unbiased, a humanitarian, and endlessly forgiving and passionate when it came to his family. The kids admired him to the end of the earth.

I knew how much it hurt him to have tumbled so far on the career ladder, after plotting his life to achieve one goal after the other, like building the walls of a brick house. We both had that feeling, that need to be everything, have everything, to never be turned down, to never be hurt or punished or disregarded. The Great Recession humbled us and poked fun at all our assumptions. We did not go down easily; instead we learned how to cope, and ten years later, we reassembled our dreams. They had morphed into something else entirely, but I think we both believed we had regressed, that we had lost something we could never get back. Sometimes I think we are still forty in our minds. We mourn the loss of those years of achievement, ten years of relative bleakness.

Jay and I approached healing in different ways. He had always landed work through his connections, and around the time I started working at Stratford, he ran into a former co-worker who drew him back into software at a company where he had to reinvent himself as a financial analyst. Numbers were not Jay's thing, but he threw himself at the role like a man headed to war who had never held a gun. Several years before, he had purchased an Excel instruction book the size of an old Yellow Pages phone book and, after several months of study, could have taught advanced Excel to college students.

He worked long hours after the kids had gone to bed, reworking spreadsheets, correcting mistakes, preparing for presentations. It all looked like rather dry and lonesome work to me, but I would have traded what I was doing at Stratford for that kind of inanity any day. We both knew that Jay was putting in his time, and his labor would lead to advancement. We had to take the steps. Our recovery from the recession was not going to be instantaneous or painless. We kept drinking martinis, adding wine at dinner on occasion, falling into bed blurry brained and depleted, and hoping for better tomorrows.

Looking back now, I can see how I coped while I worked at Stratford. I treasured my weekends, when I wasn't on call, for the chance to watch Gunnar or Camille play soccer or run cross-country, to see Cole play basketball and help

Ava make cookies in the kitchen. This was when my parent brain cleared out all the work stuff and concentrated on my children. We woke at 7 a.m. for the kids' sports and stayed up well past midnight watching *Saturday Night Live* or any other television show that made us laugh.

We sat around the dinner table, occasionally getting a word in while the kids interrupted one another with their opinions, criticisms, wild ideas, and fantasies of their future lives. We did our best to accept it all, even if inwardly we cringed or tried not to burst out laughing.

I started to do things that I recalled enjoying—cooking new recipes, taking yoga classes, and going for longer runs. We didn't have much extra cash, nor was I much of a clothes hound, so trips to the mall or lunches out were limited to when the kids were desperate for new cleats, winter jackets, or supplies for school trips. Our children were everything to us, and we reveled in their humanity, their inability to see much past any given day, to not fret, to find humor in inane things like funny-shaped vegetables, our cross-eyed dog Teeka, and the hairy earlobes of their social studies teacher at school.

And we had always had a powerful group of friends. Friends of twenty years or more, friends we had made through work, friends we met through the kids' schools and activities, and friends we picked up at our athletic club and volunteer work. Our friends kept us moving forward through dinners out, dinners in, weekday walks, weekends away, and celebrations of our children's accomplishments. We were there for one another. We saved the other from drowning, from overreacting, from giving up. In the glow of friend time, we could forget all the angst of the day.

I went to see a naturopath during this time. On top of the anxiety of work, I had started having night sweats, sleepless nights, hair loss, stomach aches, and vicious headaches. Menopause had taken hold. I found a new rheumatologist as well, a placid but strong-willed doctor who assessed me, asked me questions about my home life and how I felt. No doctor had ever asked me such questions before, and I choked on my emotions the first time I tried to answer. The doctor patted my hand like my dearest aunt used to and advised me to keep warm clothing with me at all times, in the car, in my office, in the kitchen, and so forth. Anything to help with my Raynaud's during the long winter months.

"You take hot pocket warmers with you to the soccer games, right?" she asked. "And silk underwear is good, and I have another patient who recommends this tea . . ."

The fundamental practicality of her approach silenced me. These were basic steps I, or anyone for that matter, could take toward wellness. In considering all that was written down on the "prescription" for me as I departed her office, I realized that there had been a shift in healthcare that I personally had missed, and I found it refreshing and bold. This is what they meant, I realized, as I thought of my graduate school classes, by "patient-centered care."

The irony was not lost on me that for a year and a half I had oversight to this type of care at Stratford, as each resident had an individual care plan, as unique to them as the lines on the palms of their hand. Yet while immersed in following all of the residents' plans, I failed to establish or follow my own.

I needed to treat myself as the patient. I needed to get past this setback in my own physical and mental health and get well.

30

LOSING THE PLOT

In the spring of 2018 Jay and I moved back upstairs to the master bedroom after painting it a dusky blue gray, refinishing the hardwoods, hanging a new medicine cabinet in the master bath, and rearranging art on the walls. Sitting on the edge of the bed, I looked out the large sun-filled window onto the cul-de-sac, and memories of our first years together flooded over me like the cold rush of a mountain stream.

"Nine years, I think," I spoke into the room, knowing Jay could hear me in the closet-size bathroom with the door open as he washed his face with his hands.

"Nine years we slept in the basement?" he answered. So often I would say something right after he had thought it himself, and vice versa, that we had become accustomed to short sentences with no need for elaboration.

"Yes, hard to believe. It was so cold down there. So dark. I feel like we've emerged from a cave." Like butterflies from their cocoons.

"We've made it, sweetheart," Jay answered as he came

back into the room. "We got those kids pretty much done. It's our time now."

I pondered this and felt, not for the first time as we witnessed three of our four children graduate from high school, endure the laborious process of college applications, and launch into the world, that I was waiting for something. The wait had not been restful. It was not like waiting for a friend to show up on a bench in a park or watching a leaf fall to the ground. Nor was it fearful, like those last few moments before the wheels of an airplane safely hits the tarmac while you grip the armrests of your seat.

It was more of a precarious waiting, the sort you had just before your birthday party when you were six or seven and were suddenly sure that no one would show up. As you waited nervously, shadows would cross the dining room, the lemonade would grow warm in the punch bowl, and the candles on the cake would remain unlit.

It seemed as if I'd been waiting for decades. After the divorce, I kind of lost my mind. On the outside I kept it together to be the mama my children needed, the employee my employer had come to expect, and the woman my friends and family had relied on. But somewhere between the end of the trial and the children being on the verge of leaving home, I forgot how to have fun. I lost all that was childlike and light within me, not that I had ever had much.

As my mother would say, I lost the plot.

And what was the plot?

In the most normal years, when I was somewhere between

the ages of eight and thirteen, I played board games with my friends, rode a Schwinn bike, baked endless batches of oatmeal cookies, and sat on the floor in the bedroom I shared with my older sister, cutting out pictures of models from women's magazines while the Beatles played on my cassette recorder. In those years, I never stumbled.

I don't remember crying until Caitlin moved to Seattle to dance, and suddenly our room was full of echoes. I remember meeting my friends at the Beaverton roller rink and gliding in huge circles, around and around, to the Bee Gees and Loverboy on the loudspeaker. The crystal ball and spotlights made me feel glamorous and grown up. Now and then I would let a boy hold my hand, and after a while I'd skate away from him, looking over my shoulder with a slow moving-on kind of smile.

I read countless novels and watched *60 Minutes* with my parents on Sunday nights. I filled my journals with dreams of seeing wild beasts on safari in Africa, of snorkeling in the turquoise waters off Antigua, of riding in a train across Siberia. More mundane scenarios never occurred to me, that I might find a profession, fall in love, bear children, dress them for preschool in the mornings, and offer them three cereal boxes to choose from.

It was as if I woke up and found myself, one day, at fifty. I watched her—that woman who was me—as if she were standing on a seashore with waves breaking at her feet. I watched her, felt afraid for her, and grieved for her. She was lost, I think. She was sad. How did she get here? Is there a way to go back? What could she recover as she combs through the shifting sands of her life? What did she see in there? There are flashes of colorful beach glass, broken shells, a crab's back and claws. There is the odd translucent jellyfish. There is a seagull's feather and bits of plastic litter. In front of her was an ocean of purpose and loss.

At Stratford, we were all swimming in that ocean, trying to stay afloat. Some days the ocean raged with lightning on the horizon. Other days you could have floated on a raft as if you were sunbathing, the sea calm. We strove to meet each resident's basic needs; we could do nothing more. Few residents could fight for more; they had resigned themselves to this: a bed, a chair, a toilet, a window, and a plate of food.

It made me wonder if people in prison were more satisfied with their lot. How was Stratford different from that? How was it any better?

Take the issue of the smoking porch, a problem that festered like a mosquito bite in summer. We have a right to smoke, our residents insisted, when the staff proposed to move the designated spot farther away or eliminate it altogether. I am too old/weak/disabled/unstable to go farther, they said. I need my smokes, they repeated. It's cheaper than alcohol, and would you rather we drink?

And why tell us the hours we can and cannot smoke? If I want to smoke with the raccoons messing with the garbage cans at 3 a.m., what do you care? I have the pass code to the building. I can come and go. I live here.

Yes, they lived there. And as we justified the rules—Stratford was a healthcare facility and part of a larger hospital system after all, and smoking (and alcohol consumption) contradicted our mission and core values—we reassured ourselves that for most of them it was better inside Stratford than out. When residents returned after wandering away, they were often disoriented and disheveled. The nurses sighed as they met them at the door.

"Come on, let's get you a shower and check your vitals. In fact, just pull over here, and I'll check your BP and pulse right now. What happened to your jacket? How did you get that cut above your left eye?"

Some would let the nurse take over. Others would swat their arms before giving up. Inside, other residents stopped to high-five and question those who had returned. *Where'd you go, man? What's up with your eye? Who did you see? What was it like out there?*

When the fray died down, I'd welcome the resident back, too. My desire to be kind was often muddled with dismay as I assessed what had been lost in these lives.

Long after I left Stratford I continued to wonder, when does a child cross from innocence to awareness? What does it take for once pleasurable things to become something that wounds us instead of lifting us up with joy? Why must living harden us? Experience takes a toll on us, reminds us of what we have missed and what we would never want to do again. We forget to giggle until tears are streaming from our eyes, and we forget to savor each lick of ice cream, to get up early to watch cartoons, to run barefooted on fresh-mown lawns.

I was working at trying to find the little girl I used to be. I was working at it, but I had buried her deep within me. When did she cross that bridge? She never looked back. Until after Stratford.

I sometimes drank martinis so I could sleep, and then I would wake up in the middle of the night in fear. My sleep was shallow, without nurture. I exercised almost every day, feeling nothing: no pain, no strain, no endorphins. I would sweat, shower, change my clothes. My body had no meaning to me; I didn't inspect it the way I did as a child, a teenager, a young woman, or a mother. I didn't touch it or turn this way and that in front of the mirror. I dressed and undressed as fast as possible. I was not repulsed. I was just a shell.

All of this indifference to my outer self was a combination of the experience of menopause and the physical effect of my incurable autoimmune disorders. The slow progression of my scleroderma in particular frightened me, and only by trying not to think about it too closely was I able to continue on. Silently I went about addressing the continuing evidence of the disorder—my hardening skin, my occasional shortness of breath, my numb hands and feet—by experimenting with both natural and prescribed remedies to see if they took hold. Increasingly I became aware of the impact my state of mind had on the disorder's existence, and, as I did, I focused more and more on my mind. My mind was the only thing that would save my body from attacking itself.

When I read novels, there was a rare connection to the author's words. Oh yes! My heart and mind ignited. Suddenly

I was like a girl sprinting upstairs to meet a friend. Then, at the top I would catch my breath, and the excitement was all behind me.

I would get jittery having to sit at a desk all day. I flexed and stretched my leg muscles and stood up to go to the bathroom just to move. When I came home, I wanted to stand. I did housework, cooked, and stepped from one room to the next. The dog watched me with her curious, crossed eyes. Could she appreciate how I felt? She was old and slept most of the day, snoring and making small yelps when she dreamed.

During the weekend I could finally try and sleep. I didn't have to put on makeup and could wear my hair pulled back. I could linger at the gourmet food shop, choosing cheeses and charcuteries. I could do yoga and practice "watching my breath." I could talk to my children on FaceTime and not be in a hurry.

Sometimes I allowed myself to do something different. I would go on a hike in the woods or wander through the art museum. I met one of my parents for coffee. I called my sister. I attended open houses for homes I couldn't afford to buy. It felt indulgent, and I wondered if I might get caught. Then I thought, *Who cares what I do?* And that thought brought tears to my eyes. I *knew* people cared. What was wrong with me? People cared. Heat rushed through me as though I were standing by a bonfire. I was full of contradictions. I was starving but only wanted hot tea. I couldn't explain why I didn't really like my new job. I couldn't explain most things;

it was as if my brain had become overwrought, tender, full of holes.

As I tried to put it all into perspective, I realized it wasn't just me. This happens to the universe of women. At a certain age we lose the plot. We are unhappy. We feel as though we are losing our minds. The art of living, the act of living, is something we no longer accomplish with ease. We can't seem to bounce back. We don't know what we want, who we want, how we should be. I kept hoping to see the path in the woods, the light in the forest, the cabin that is the source of the light. There, maybe all would become clear again.

I was right. Given time, we do rediscover the path.

31

UPROOTED

One of the things I took away from working at Stratford was an appreciation for a place to call "home." Homelessness has spread like wildfire across several cities, including Portland, and become a topic of deep concern. Stratford was one of the best homes many of our residents had ever had. Despite its many failings, it still provided a haven—a safe, warm, and comforting place where you could sleep fearlessly, eat copiously, and bathe when you felt unclean. At Stratford you could follow a routine and spend enough time with someone that you began to care for them.

Memories of the places my family called home are wrapped up in the squares of a quilt that my mother made from old clothes. Other reminiscences are evoked by the black-and-white photos my father or a friend took of my siblings and me as we grew. I can hold one in my hand like a Tarot card, and images from the past spring up.

I asked my mother to remind me of the names of streets we lived on because I have forgotten most of them. I was born in Eugene, where we lived first on Emerald and then on Oak Street, then a street she couldn't recall in Northeast Portland. In Cambridge, the halfway house was on Marie Avenue. After that we moved to Northwest Northrup Street in Portland, and we finally landed at Southwest Seventy-Fifth, in the only house my parents ever owned together.

As we moved from one home to another, we left many things behind and took little. When we broke apart, I held on to images of the things that stayed the same: my mother at her sewing machine, my father at his typewriter, my brother making music, and my sister wrapped up in her bed with sweets and stuffed animals.

I had my books, my journals, my addiction to food, and my dreams of living in fancy houses with marble floors. We had family vacations camping with sleeping bags that smelled of campfire and marshmallows. At the Oregon coast we stayed in damp beach houses with creaking floorboards gritty with sand.

My family was a family that told stories, often conceived in the moment but just as frequently spun from the past. We swapped tales over the dinner table and teased each other about silly, scary, inane, and bizarre things that we did long ago. My parents would drink wine or scotch, my mother's long arms pointing this way and that as she narrated. My father would observe her, often on the verge of laughter.

"No, Sandra, that's not what happened," he'd say, and my mother would look at us kids with feigned innocence.

"Well, that's the way I remember it," she'd say in her

actress tone. My father would start his own version of the
story, as Josh and Caitlin squirmed in their chairs, eager to
participate. My mother says I used to sit there with my hands
folded together, waiting diligently for the punch line.

Thus, home for me is family, not a place. I felt unat-
tached to the physical places I lived in growing up. I was
never taught how to make a home; rather, I learned how
to make the best of my surroundings. This was clarified to
me in a recent conversation about homelessness with my
mother. "People need a *place*, not a *home* per se," she said.
I looked at her, her feet up on a stool, tea by her side, various blankets, pillows, and a bookstand, as well as her nail
file and knitting, all within reach. She was adept at arrang-
ing herself in place.

It has taken me half my life to learn how to transform
the place I lived in into the home I wanted it to be. Perhaps
I wasn't sure I had a right to say how I wanted it to be. Up
until the point I started living with Jay, every choice I made
around nesting seemed to stem from an economic trigger. I
simply agreed to designs preferred by my partner or my children or my parents.

Five-year-old Camille wanted her bedroom pink and purple, so that was what I painted it. My furniture was inherited
from my parents. It was old to start with and had been
acquired from relatives, neighbors, estate sales, and antique
shops. One boyfriend bought me several framed prints that
he admired and believed suited me (they did), while another
helped me pick light fixtures and bathroom tiles. A realtor

suggested dark granite for my kitchen remodel, and I found a deeply discounted box at Home Depot and used it.

When I did choose some bit of décor on my own, the decision felt tentative, like taking vows I feared would be broken. I focused on the things that brought me comfort: a solid cherry bed frame, a handcrafted bookshelf for the living room, a good reading light, and vases full of flowers on the dining table. (The table itself and the chairs were passed on to me by my father's second wife and couldn't have cost more than two hundred dollars new. They lasted the entire eighteen years we lived on Washington Street.)

Many people furnish their home this way. There were residents at Stratford, who acquired furniture abandoned on the sidewalk and makeshift shelving from discarded orange crates. I also know people who redesign their living room every seven years and only buy things new. I wonder how they have any attachment to all these new things.

I have kept some things my whole life, moving them from the house I grew up in to my college dorm to the first apartment Scott and I rented to the house I live in now. They are simple objects—a gold chain that hangs over my vanity mirror, a two-inch, round-framed photo of my brother and me when we were three and one. Classic books I can't bear to part with, a wool hat knit by my mother, a favorite coffee mug. Their mere existence in my house signals that I am home.

Jay was the first person to listen to me describe what I wanted in a home. For years, he and I had to make do with the 1,960 square feet of space on Washington Street. Once the kids were off to college, long after my time at Stratford and well into our next, more fulfilling careers, it was as though my blinders came off. I started to notice just how many things I wanted to change, and I started asking myself, *Why not?*

I was fifty! I raised four kids! I had autoimmune disorders. I survived an awful divorce, Stratford, and the Great Recession. Jay heard me and started making lists and spreadsheets, and the designer in him started drawing plans to redo the house we lived in. Instead, I told him we needed to move. He crumpled up his papers, and we began looking at houses. We looked and looked until we were cross-eyed from looking.

I focused on what I wanted: a larger kitchen, a real dining room, a real master bedroom and master bath. I dreamed about sunlit living rooms, rose gardens, vast closets. I churned through email after email of new home listings, scoffing at people's poor taste, considering ways to rearrange kitchens and knock down walls to let in the light. I dragged Jay to open houses every weekend for most of a year. Our enthusiasm waxed and waned as we grew excited by photos online only to discover that the houses looked nothing like the pictures. Or else there was the smell of cat urine, a postage-stamp yard, a minuscule master bath, an impossibly steep driveway, aluminum windows, and teensy bedrooms with even teensier closets.

Jay would not allow us to settle. *We will find IT, or we will stay put* seemed to be his motto, as we sat at the bar in our kitchen, having heard our realtor tell us for the third time our offer on a house had been outbid.

And then one afternoon in April, everything changed. It was like hearing you got into the college of your choice, after all. We returned to the second house we had looked at six months earlier. It had been pulled from the market when it didn't sell. And now we laid fresh eyes on what came to be known as the Hawthorne House. We had our realtor ask the owner if it was still for sale. Indeed, it was. It had been waiting for us, all this time. Our home.

32

ROOTED

We are at dinner with my mother, Jay, my father, and his wife, Liz. It is my father's seventy-fifth birthday, and we are eating steak. My father had found a more congenial match in his second marriage. After drifting for a couple of years, he gave up teaching for a career as a stockbroker. He and Liz married in 2005, at the University Club, where Jay and I later had our own wedding ceremony.

I am not drinking this evening, because I am on a self-imposed ninety-day alcohol-free challenge. I am on day sixty-seven. It has not been hard. My father apologizes to me for drinking a martini right next to me. I tell him it doesn't ruffle me, and it really doesn't. Jay drinks red wine, and my mother has Perrier, perhaps in solidarity with me or perhaps because she's already taken some pain pills for her bum leg. Liz has a martini, like my father, and then they move on to chardonnay.

Red wine doesn't treat him as well as it used to, my father says. I want to pat his hand in commiseration. He took wine-tasting classes in the 1970s, when such things were just starting to be hip in Portland.

For some reason the conversation turns to my growing up. My mother tells Jay how many times I called home crying for her and my father to let me come back. She looks at my father across the table for confirmation, but he doesn't respond. Either he hasn't heard her or he's trying to help me maintain my dignity.

"There was the Y camp; what was it? Westwind? You hated the canteen-style food; you hated the moldy cabins."

"Everyone else knew each other there and had been coming every summer for years," I retort.

I am mildly bemused. My mother goes on.

"Then there was Europe. That was awful."

I look at her, wondering who exactly it was awful for. "Mom, I really enjoyed Europe. The first time. The bike trip though Germany, you remember?"

At this point, although Jay, my father, and Liz are watching us, only my mother and I are speaking, exchanging words like a tennis volley. My mother smacks the ball back over the net.

"Right, I guess so. But France, that was not a happy time for you."

"You're right, Mom, it was not. I had no money. French people are mean, and initially I had a terrible living situation . . ." Even to my ears this all sounds pathetic and silly. I am now fifty-one, after all.

My mother waves her hand at me, her regular gesture that meant *stop being so silly*. Liz coughs and tries to change the subject, while murmuring, "That sounds awful," under her breath. Jay says nothing, nor does my father. My mother still has that kind of influence at the dinner table.

Our steaks arrive, along with warnings from the wait staff about the hot plates. The conversation turns to talk of my father's recent hospital tests, the latest in a long line of them after a heart attack a few years back. He has never quite regained his strength.

My mother tends to bounce back more thoroughly from her own health setbacks, chiseling away at recovery week by week until she has returned to as close a version of her former self as she can be.

In their idiosyncratic approach to aging, my parents are not unlike the population I dealt with at Stratford. They are definitely two of the lucky ones, though, still living in their own homes, still driving cars, still coming and going on their own schedules, with no one knocking at their door to deliver medication and check their pulse.

This topic of my crying to come home throughout my childhood reminded me of the way I dealt with working at Stratford, which was an imperfect but welcome home for its residents. As I spent my days there, all the loss, trauma, and fear I had experienced—in being told to go away from home, in being carried away from home, in being introduced to a new home, in being asked to call a new place home, in trying to make a home for myself, my partners, and my children—rose up and knocked me over like a wave.

Home for me was never the haven it was drummed up to

be; it was the place I came to at night, where I searched for the solace I only sometimes found. It was walls and doors and light fixtures and creaky, clunky, ticky sounds in the night. It was my brother's band playing in the basement, my mother crying in her bed, my father asleep on the couch, dirty dishes in the sink. It was living with plastic-covered windows and doorways through the chill of a Portland winter, and plaster dust, cigarette smoke, and fresh paint when I was nine months pregnant.

At Stratford new carpet was often stained after only a week; people's belongings were dropped into hallways and trampled indifferently. There was a constant cycle of acute illness, angry confrontations, and tears. Yet there was the recognition that this was perhaps the best home some residents had ever known.

At Stratford I recognized both my privilege and my revulsion at the disconnect between my desire to help and my aching need to escape.

I have always been told I am brave, I am strong. I almost died as an infant, my mother likes to say; our mismatched blood caused jaundice that gave my tiny body the color of melted butter. For three weeks, my parents left me at the hospital where the nurses directed a heat lamp at me.

I am brave, my parents told themselves so that they could keep pushing me out in the world toward all the things that frightened me. So that I would come back, they hoped, with more tough tissue, with more fortitude, and the will to keep moving forward.

And I do have tough tissue now; I have scleroderma.

I am a survivor, they told me. I am brave. I can see now how this is true; I am no longer fighting through the webs of my past that kept me from seeing the truth of that statement. Everything is so much clearer now, and I believe it.

As this book went to print, one of my dearest friends took her own life. The pain she felt must have been insurmountable. I have spent many days replaying the years we had together in friendship, centered around the rearing of our children, and our approaching middle age. I can never do or say enough to honor her memory and the determined, bright, loyal woman she was, but I can affirm she will be in my heart forever. All my love to you, Annette.

ABOUT THE AUTHOR

ERIN STAMMER grew up in Portland, Oregon, and graduated from Brown University with a bachelor of arts in comparative literature and French. She later obtained her master's in healthcare administration from Portland State University. She is married and has four grown children. When she is not reading and writing, she works full-time for a finance company, cooks, practices yoga, and enjoys traveling the world.

For an accompanying readers guide, please see

ERINSTAMMER.COM

Made in the USA
Las Vegas, NV
19 August 2021

28411368R00166